Everyday Wellbeing for Early Years Educators

Are you an early years educator struggling to find time for your own wellbeing? This guide offers simple, accessible ideas that can be incorporated into your everyday life without requiring extra money or energy – whether you have five minutes, twenty minutes or longer.

Inside, you'll discover a treasure trove of wellbeing practices tailored to your needs, from stress-relieving techniques and nature-based activities to exercise tips, creative pursuits and nourishing recipes. Learn how to make wild garlic soda bread, find peaceful walking spots, start running safely or create homemade bath salts. Each chapter offers guidance for embedding wellbeing into your routine, with actionable advice, real stories from early years educators across the UK and thoughtful suggestions for integrating these practices into both your professional and personal life.

Designed to be picked up, dipped into and applied immediately, *Everyday Wellbeing for Early Years Educators* is an invaluable resource for all professionals working with young children. By prioritising these small moments of self-care, you'll not only enhance your own wellbeing but also strengthen your capacity to nurture and support the children in your setting.

Sonia Mainstone-Cotton is a freelance nurture specialist and Thrive Licenced Practitioner working with Brighter Futures Nurture Outreach team, she has extensive experience of working in schools and early years settings with children who have high social, emotional and mental health needs. Sonia also delivers training across the country, working with early years settings, charities and schools.

"This outstanding book from Sonia is an absolute treasure for everyone on their wellbeing journey – wherever you are on that journey. The refreshing practicality that Sonia has woven throughout makes this book unique in the wellbeing arena. Whether you have five minutes or a full afternoon, you'll find recipes, nature walks, planting suggestions, exercise ideas and more that you can genuinely fit into your life.

Rooted in research and drawing on a rich variety of mental health and wellbeing sources, this evidence-based book manages to feel warm, supportive, and wholeheartedly human. Sonia has thoughtfully addressed diversity and ethnicity, acknowledging that wellbeing doesn't look or feel the same for everyone. This refreshing honesty makes the book truly inclusive.

The anecdotes and vignettes from real people that you will find featured in each chapter are thought-provoking and engaging. The underlying celebration of family and friends – from small acts such as cooking together to full days out – are a wonderful reminder that wellbeing is something we can nurture together. This is a great book to keep to hand for your everyday wellbeing ideas."

– **Kathy Brodie**, Founder of Early Years TV

"*Everyday Wellbeing* is an easy to read, practical book which encourages everyone to consider how they can better take care of themselves. There is such a rich range of ideas included. Many individulas have shared experiences of their own chosen activities to boost their wellbeing; these were both interseting and inspirational. I really enjoyed having a go at one of the wellbeing exercises at the end of each chapter. It was helpful that there were suggestions of activities of differing lengths depending on what time I had available. This book will be benificail to anyone reading it and I will be recommending it to educators I work with as well as family and friends."

– **Sharon Cooke**, Thrive Licensed Practitioner,
Nurture Specialist and Author

Everyday Wellbeing for Early Years Educators

Simple and Sustainable Wellbeing Practices

Sonia Mainstone-Cotton

Routledge
Taylor & Francis Group
LONDON AND NEW YORK

Designed cover image: Ian Cotton

First published 2027
by Routledge
4 Park Square, Milton Park, Abingdon, Oxon OX14 4RN

and by Routledge
605 Third Avenue, New York, NY 10158

Routledge is an imprint of the Taylor & Francis Group, an informa business

British Library Cataloguing-in-Publication Data
A catalogue record for this book is available from the British Library

ISBN: 9781041207085 (hbk)
ISBN: 9781041207078 (pbk)
ISBN: 9781003717591 (ebk)

DOI: 10.4324/9781003717591

Typeset in Optima LT Std
by Apex CoVantage, LLC

So many people have contributed to this book, thank you to everyone who offered ideas for walks, recipes, tips on how they support their wellbeing, ideas around exercise and shared what brings them joy. Thank you for putting up with me asking, reminding and asking you again! I hugely appreciate your input.

Contents

Introduction

Thank you for picking up this book and dipping in. My name is Sonia, and I work for a small multi-disciplinary team in Bath and North East Somerset called Brighter Futures. We work with children who have high social, emotional and mental health needs. In our role, we have the privilege of working with children in nurseries and primary schools and the adults who support them. I first wrote a book about staff wellbeing in 2017 (*Promoting Wellbeing in Early Years Staff*). Since then, the world of wellbeing and early years has shifted and developed; thankfully, our understanding of wellbeing practice has increased. You may be wondering why another book on this subject, which is a good question! Along with supporting staff and children in school, I deliver training across the country on the subject of wellbeing. Over the years, I have noticed that many people want practical, easy suggestions and ideas. That's what I hope to share in this book. This is a step sideways from lots of theory about wellbeing and a step towards ideas and practice.

I will look at the overall theme of wellbeing in this introduction, but then the rest of the book will look at some specific areas, and each section will be full of practical ideas. This book is about supporting the wellbeing of adults, but at the end of each chapter, I have a small section on how we could embed some of the ideas into our practice with the children we work with or in our families. At the end of each chapter, I will share a section which offers ideas if you have 5 minutes, 10 minutes, 20 minutes or 40 minutes.

When I am delivering wellbeing training, I often describe the session as a menu of ideas. I would like you to see this book in that way: there will be some things on the menu that are not for you, other areas you might like to try and others you are keen to give a go. At different times in our lives, we need different elements to support us. I hope this book will enable you to find some things that can support you.

DOI: 10.4324/9781003717591-1

I work in nurseries and primary schools, but also have many friends who work in social care, senior schools and youth settings. The one similar strand for all of us is that we work in increasingly difficult times, our workloads often feel bigger and harder, and we may feel an increase in demands on us. Some of those things we might be able to change, but many we probably can't. But there are some things we can do, and one of them is taking care of ourselves. This book will offer a range of suggestions on ways to do that.

Development of the idea of wellbeing

When I first wrote the staff wellbeing book in 2017, it was one of the first on the market around the subject of wellbeing for early years staff. The term wellbeing was being talked about a little, but I wouldn't say it was embedded in the public's minds and practice. Since then, there has been an increase in understanding, knowledge and practice in this area. I am the series advisor for The Little Minds Matter series with Routledge. This series has the overall theme of children's wellbeing. One of those books is by Kate Moxley, titled *A Guide to Mental Health for Early Years* (2022). This is an excellent book; Kate is a trainer for mental health first aid, and in this book she explores our mental health, how to recognise when we are mentally unwell and how to find support for this. Her book is an essential one for our sector.

Along with the development in understanding of wellbeing in the education sector, it has also become a hugely growing development in the rest of life. There are growing number of books, groups and podcasts on the subject, in many ways that is brilliant, however I do have a slight concern that the arena of wellbeing can leave many feeling this is for middle-class white people, who have time, who have money, who have resources, and some people jump to the conclusion this is not for me. I would like to address that and explore how we can all access wellbeing ideas, without needing lots of money or time to do so.

Many in the early years sector are female. To give you an idea of this, in 2023, the Department of Education found that there were 259,300 staff working in group-based settings (nurseries) and 55,800 in school-based provision (nursery class in school), and 32,200 childminders: 98% of the staff were female in groups and schools, and 97% childminders were female, 83% were white British in settings and 82% of childminders. We also know that early years staff are often on the lowest incomes in demanding jobs. In 2023, the Education Committee published its report on support for childcare and early years. They identified several problems in the early years workforce:

- difficulty recruiting qualified staff
- a lack of professional development
- low pay
- long hours
- low status

Interestingly, what they haven't identified within that list is that so few men work in the sector, and it is a predominantly white workforce. Both of these need addressing; we know we need children to see people like them who work with them, both through gender and colour. For more on these issues, do look at an interview with Jamel Carly Campbell on the Tapestry podcasts and look at Liz Pemberton, The Black Nursery Manager website. On her website, she has an excellent video she has made with Barnardo's. Because we are a predominantly female workforce that is often paid poorly, it is easy to presume that wellbeing is a luxury and one we don't have time to engage in or be part of. Through all my writing and training and 1:1 work with staff, I try hard to demonstrate and show that wellbeing is something we can all be part of, we can all do something that will help us.

Why focus on wellbeing

For the last 12 years, I have honed and worked on my wellbeing and supporting others' wellbeing. I learnt early on in the role with Brighter Futures that if I didn't care for myself, then I couldn't care well for the children I was supporting. I know, and I have learnt I can only do my best with children when I feel good in myself, which is part of loving myself. I believe that at the heart of self-wellbeing is loving ourselves. I think it is crucial to recognise that I matter, I need to love myself, care for myself and nurture myself, and this is not a luxury, it is a fundamental need. Of course, that doesn't mean that there haven't been times during the last 12 years when I haven't been anxious or struggled with my mental health, but I have found the things that help me, and for that I am very thankful.

This is not about mental illness support

Before proceeding with this, I just want to acknowledge and identify that I am not suggesting for a moment that sitting in the garden looking at a flower, or having a hot bath at the end of the day, is going to sort out all your problems. I am also not suggesting that if you do a few wellbeing activities, then you will stay mentally well all the time. There are times when we will have difficulties with our mental health, and many of us will become mentally unwell. The charity Mind suggests that 1 in 4 people in the UK will experience a mental health problem of some kind in the UK each year. It is so important that we recognise when we are becoming mentally unwell and that we seek help with this. At the end of this chapter, there are some organisations with expert advice on this. Also, look at Kate Moxley's book or better still, go on her training; her website is listed below.

This is about practical steps

I have explained what this book is not, but what I am hoping to offer you is a range of ideas and suggestions, from myself, but also many other people across the country. In this book, I will bring in different stories of how people take small steps to support themselves. There may be ideas you have heard before and do yourself, but I am hoping there will also be some ideas that are new and you might like to give them a go. On different days, we need different things. Sometimes, the best wellbeing practice I can do is allow myself to have a short nap at the end of the work day, other days getting into cold water is the boost I need.

Each chapter will offer ideas, tips and suggestions that you can use in everyday life, that you can fit in around your work, family and other commitments. My aim for this book is that it will bring in not just the theory and ideas, but also the practices. I will be sharing places to walk, spots to swim, recipes to try, foraging ideas and apps to download to identify wildlife. I hope to make this a really practical book. The emphasis is on how we can embed wellbeing practices, rather than having them as a one-off to do in the holidays or on the nursery wellbeing week, but instead about making habits that help us. Some ideas will cost some money, but lots won't. I recognise that I am a white, middle-class, middle-aged woman living in Somerset. I am aware this brings with it huge privileges; for that reason, I am working hard to include the voices and experiences of many people who work in our sector across the UK, so it won't be just my ideas. But of course, this will largely be my voice and my experiences that I am sharing with you based on practices I use and try regularly.

References

Childcare workforce in England: https://commonslibrary.parliament.uk/research-briefings/cbp-9948/

Liz Pemberton: https://www.theblacknurserymanager.com/

Mind: https://www.mind.org.uk/information-support/types-of-mental-health-problems/mental-health-facts-and-statistics/

Moxley, K. (2022) *A Guide to Mental Health for Early Years Educators.* Routledge.

Kate Moxley: https://katemoxleyeyc.co.uk/

Support for childcare and the early years – Report summary: https://publications.parliament.uk/pa/cm5803/cmselect/cmeduc/969/summary.html

Jamel interview: Tapestry podcasts- https://fsf-podcasts.simplecast.com/episodes/the-early-years-is-the-jewel-in-our-communitys-crown-jamel-carly-campbell

1 Stress

I decided I needed to start this book with a chapter on stress. Stress is an area we all talk about; it's no longer the taboo subject it used to be, but I also wonder if sometimes we talk about how very stressed we are as a badge of honour, to prove that we are working hard. I know in the past I have been guilty of that. Some stress is fine; we all need a bit of stress to get up in the morning and arrive at work on time. At times, stress can be beneficial to us; stress on the body can release adrenaline, which helps our bodies fight infections. Stress can also allow us to perform at our best, such as in an interview or an exam. But the problem can be when stress builds in our bodies, when we live with it for an extended time, and we don't find ways to let it go. I suspect the feeling and experience of stress on our bodies is something we often choose to ignore.

Moment for reflection

Before we explore the topic of stress further, I want to pause and think about how you recognise when you're stressed and what the signs are in your body. Our bodies are remarkably good at signalling the impact stress is having on our bodies, but we are not always very good at noticing or listening to these signs and warnings. Take a moment to stop and consider: how does your body show you that you're stressed?

DOI: 10.4324/9781003717591-2

The website Mind has a useful page about how stress can make you feel, which includes:

Being impatient, angry, irritable
A sense of feeling overwhelmed
Feeling nervous or anxious
A sense of foreboding or dread
Little interest in life, feeling there is no enjoyment in life
Feeling worried and tense

The physical signs of stress can be:
Tight chest and difficulty breathing
Panic attacks
Sleep problems
Deep tiredness
Headaches and muscle aches
Chest pain and high blood pressure
Heartburn and indigestion
Constipation and diarrhoea (sometimes people describe having IBS symptoms)
Feeling dizzy, faint or sick
Sudden weight gain or loss
Changes to your period

We will all experience different warnings from our bodies. The key is knowing your warnings. My main signs are having tense shoulders leading to migraines. Being irritable and intolerant, feeling anxious and having a strong craving to be alone. Over the years, I have got better at recognising the signs, but sometimes they still creep up, and it takes a close friend or my husband/daughter to name it.

Cortisol

Cortisol is a hormone in our body. Sometimes it is described as our body's alarm system. When we are under stress, the hormone works with our brain to impact our mood, motivation and fear. It's the hormone that kicks into action when we are in fight/flight. Cortisol is a useful hormone, as it also helps regulate our sleep-wake cycle, aids in the body's use of fats, carbohydrates and proteins, and can provide the boost we need to manage a stressful situation. The problem is when we are constantly stressed, and cortisol levels remain high, when we haven't found ways to release the cortisol. If cortisol levels stay high in our body, this can lead to weight gain, anxiety, heart problems, high blood sugar, difficulty concentrating, brain fog and sleep problems.

The cause and potential consequences of stress

Sometimes we know the cause of stress, and we can actively take steps to eliminate it; most of the time, the cause is not something we can easily get rid of. If finances are tight, a new bill comes in, we may find we can't easily sort those. If we're about to go for a hospital appointment or awaiting medical results, we can't remove that wait or the feelings with it; we may find stress in the workplace due to workload, and again, this is not necessarily easily fixed. Dr Julie Smith, who is a GP and has written an excellent book, *Why has nobody told me this before* (2022), expresses unease at the idea that we just need to reduce stress in our lives. She suggests that many of the stresses we experience are non-negotiable and proposes that we need to find ways to process them and release the effects they are having on our bodies.

There are many books on the market which address stress, and some will give the impression that it only takes a few simple exercises and practices, and you will eliminate the stress. I am very wary about these, and on the whole, I look to people with some medical knowledge and research, and I generally avoid any celebrities or influencers on this! One person I have found useful is Dr Rangan Chatrejee; he has a podcast (link at end of the chapter) and several books, and I particularly like his early book, *The stress solution* (2018). It's a few years old now, but I still find it a useful book; it's a great dip in and out of, easy-to-read book with lots of pictures. Dr Rangan is a GP, and throughout the book, he talks about how he has seen the impact stress has on many of his patients. He suggests that stress can have serious long-term consequences for our health.

He also suggests that too often we are blasé about stress and do not take it seriously enough.

Both Dr Chatterjee and Dr Smith discuss the need for us to each have a toolkit to manage stress and release it from our bodies. In 2020, Brené Brown interviewed two sisters, Emily and Amelia Nagoski, who wrote a book called *Burnout*, and the interview explored their ideas around how to daily release stress from our bodies. In their interview and book, they discuss how sometimes we can identify the stress, maybe even eliminate the stressor, but we also need to actively release the stress from our bodies. They propose we need to do this daily.

Releasing stress

All of the writers mentioned above offer similar ideas on how to release stress from our bodies. These include

Exercise
Time in nature
Mindfulness
Being creative
Time with others
Intimacy

The Nagoski sisters also suggest laughing or crying as good stress relievers. Research shows that emotional tears contain cortisol, meaning you are releasing some cortisol through crying. Also, crying stimulates the parasympathetic nervous system (sometimes called rest and digest), and it counteracts the effects of the sympathetic nervous system (fight/flight). Crying can help to move us into a more relaxed state. If you would like to understand this more, there is a page on the NeuroLaunch website explaining in more detail.

I like how these appear as a menu of ideas, and that each day we can ask ourselves which is the stress release I need today. Sometimes for me the stress relief I need is getting home from work and sitting in the garden for 10 minutes with a cup of chamomile tea; other times it is listening to a podcast that I know will make me laugh or watching a comedy I find funny; other days I know the only thing that will release the stress is being in cold water in nature (see the chapter on exercise for more on this).

Did you know?

Stress may impact how often you get sick, as chronic stress can contribute to a weaker immune system

Self-compassion

Along with these ideas, all the writers mentioned above explore how important it is to be kind to ourselves when we are going through a time of high stress. Often, the default can be to jump to a critical inner voice. Kirsten Neff is a leading voice on being kind and self-compassionate. I have found her work so helpful. She proposes we need to speak to ourselves when we are struggling in the way we would speak to a friend, with kindness, care, warmth and support, whereas lots of people often speak to themselves in a harsh, critical way. She suggests that when we learn to speak to ourselves more kindly, it helps us to deal better with the stressful/difficult situations we are in. In my experience, this takes practice, but I have really noticed how helpful it has been to my mental health by making this adjustment. A useful exercise she suggests in her book *Self-compassion* (2011) is to write a letter to yourself about the situation you're in, but write it as if you're writing to a friend, think about what advice you would give to the friend and write that to yourself. This may not sound much, but it is a very powerful exercise to do.

An idea from Kirsten that I use a lot both for myself and recommend in training and with staff teams is using hand massage as a way to bring down our stress levels, to give ourselves a moment of kindness and gentleness. When you are pressing on the palm of your hand, this is releasing oxytocin in your brain and lowering cortisol levels, both of which will help to lower your stress levels. Kristen Neff's website has some useful links, ideas and videos. Link to this at the end of the chapter.

Moment for reflection

Just for a moment, take a break and give yourself a hand massage using some hand cream, or if you don't have any nearby, you can still do this without. Do this intentionally and slowly, paying attention to be gentle and kind to yourself.

Smell

With all the ideas above, I would add another one that I find helps me to find some calm, and that is smell, but it has to be the right smell! I have a strong sense of smell, and some things I find hugely repulsive, but natural smells, such as herbs, I can find helpful. I grow lots of herbs in my garden, and I often walk through, grazing my hand through the mint, lavender, rosemary and oregano. Some of these smells are associated more with waking and alertness, others with calmness. I think it is the mix of a sensory hit along with nature and being outside that I find so helpful. Each year, I make lavender bags that I use with the children I work with. I have one in the car and my bag, and I often pass them on to the staff.

Lavender bag

Ingredients

1 small cotton drawstring bag
Dried lavender flowers

Instructions

Find a small cotton bag and fill it with dried lavender flowers (you can buy these online). Keep it in your bag/car/desk, or under your pillow at night. If you don't like the smell of lavender, try dried chamomile flowers instead. They last for around a year before the scent begins to fade.

Did you know?

Lavender was used in Roman times; it was burnt in bathhouses to support bathers' health, and there is evidence that they made lavender sachets to go into pillows in Medieval times

Stress toolkit

One idea I have found helpful over the years is having a toolkit for stress/wellbeing. I have found this to be a practical and helpful resource. When we are in the middle of a stress period, it can sometimes be hard to remember what helps us. If we create a toolkit when we are feeling calm and less stressed, this can be either a physical toolkit or a page of ideas; we can turn to this when our minds are feeling full and we are feeling overwhelmed. In my training sessions, I often encourage people to ask themselves the question *What do you need in your tool kit?* and encourage them to create one. In the team I work with, we all have a wellbeing toolkit, which has stress-releasing ideas as well as calming ideas. In our role of supporting children with high Social, Emotional and Mental Health (SEMH) needs, we often talk about creating a tool kit for the children we work with, with calming and releasing ideas that will support the individual child (for more ideas on this, see my previous books *Help, what do I do now* (2025) or *Supporting children with social, emotional and mental health needs in the early years* (2021)). It's the same for us.

This is an example of my toolkit:

- Coffee first thing in the morning
- Chamomile tea and water throughout the day
- Lavender sachet in my bag and car
- Hand cream for hand massage in my bag and car
- Swimming costume (both for pool and wild swimming)
- My garden/walk in nature
- Connection to friends and family
- Books
- Creating something

Moment for reflection

Just for a moment, stop and think about what you need in your tool kit. You might want to physically collect things, you may want to make a photo page on your computer/phone to remind you, or you may want to write a list and put it on the fridge/wall where you will see it regularly.

Stress relievers

In the next section of the chapter, I will be exploring some stress relievers. I will be sharing ideas of what I find useful and examples from others.

Being outside

I have learnt that being in nature almost always immediately brings down my stress levels, I feel myself breathing more deeply and slowing down. I live in a small village in Somerset, which used to be a miners' village. It has a community meadow at the back of our house. It was created for the miners and their families to have a space of recreation. This is my go-to space if I can't get to cold water. If I only have 10 minutes, I know this will bring me the breathing space I need. During the lockdowns, I walked this space every morning to see the sunrise. Over the years, I have seen hares, owls, buzzards, red kites and many different small birds and the occasional duck! (I have no idea why ducks sometimes visit, as there is no water in the meadow.) I know the space well, knowing where to find the orchids and violets, knowing when the beech trees will drop their leaves (they are always the last) and knowing when the conkers will be ready to discover on the floor. Sometimes I will walk the meadow barefoot if I need extra help in de-stressing. I find barefoot walking soothing, slowing and mindful.

Awe and wonder

Linked with walking in nature is the idea of being captured by a sense of awe and wonder. Think about the way children can be fascinated and excited, and have a sense of awe when they see a snail. Awe is an emotion, but it is one that has received less research until relatively recently. Awe occurs when we see or experience something, and it can almost feel like our breath is taken away. In the book *How to winter* (2024), the author Keri Leibowitz explores how we can engage in awe and wonder more to help us manage winter differently (if you're someone who finds winter hard, I really recommend this book). She describes a study led by Professor Virginia Sturm at the University of California. She led a study to see if people can deliberately cultivate daily awe in their lives. In the study, people in their sixties, seventies and eighties were asked to take an outdoor walk for just 15 minutes. One group needed to just walk, the other group needed to take awe walks; they were asked to try to tap into the childlike wonder we have all had. Over eight weeks, the awe walkers were reported to have experienced joy and to have had an increase in positive emotions. She goes on to suggest that awe can help us to feel a greater sense of life satisfaction, to feel more connected to those and the world around us, and it is linked to lower feelings of stress.

We often think about experiencing awe with large, magnificent things, such as seeing the northern lights or finding a beautiful and secluded beach. However, Keri Leibowitz suggests that if we re-engage our child's sense of awe, we can be captured by awe in the small moments, too. I know that I often have a sense of awe when I see a beautiful sunrise or notice a hare or the red kites in our village. Keri encourages us to notice the small details. It may be on your next walk that you notice some flowers growing in an unexpected place, or you see a bee or butterfly for the first time in the year. I think in the early years, we are good at helping children notice things. How often do we comment on the animals we see as we walk/drive past. (I still do this, and my children are 26 and 28!) Maybe we can also channel some of that awe for ourselves.

One of the best examples I saw of engaging with awe and wonder was on a study trip to a Danish Kindergarten. As well as inspiring me to forage (I have talked about this in Chapter 2), they also had a cabinet of awe and wonder, natural items that staff and children had found; this included shells, pebbles, pressed flowers and a few dead creatures! They also had animals such as a fox and an owl that had been found in the woods and sent to a taxidermist. I haven't yet got a stuffed animal, but my house has many shells, pebbles, crab shells and a beautiful dried-out starfish.

Moment for reflection

Just for a moment, think about a recent time when you were captured by a sense of awe, notice how remembering it makes you feel.

Gardening

I am adding this under stress relievers as it was one of my top three stress relievers, along with being in nature (obviously, the two are linked) and cold-water swimming. In Chapter 2, there is a bigger section on gardening. My experience is that when I am gardening, planting, weeding, potting or pottering in the greenhouse, I quickly switch off from whatever is in my head. I can lose hours when I am in the garden and find I haven't thought once about work/family/home. My mind has been completely taken up with the task of gardening, and I always feel calmer (unless the slugs and snails have been causing a rampage!). I am particularly interested in how many plants can be really beneficial in supporting our wellbeing. One of these is lavender. The English Lavender plant is particularly hardy and a good one to grow in the UK. They grow in pots or in the ground, bees and butterflies love them, and the smell is amazing. I have lots of lavender plants across my garden, most of them by pathways, so each time I walk past them, I can experience their scent. Below are ways I like to use lavender.

Lavender recipes

Lavender lemonade

This is a lovely, refreshing and soothing drink.

You will need

2 tbsp of dried lavender flowers or around 20 stems of fresh lavender flowers

2 lemons
1 l of boiled water
2 tbsp honey (or more if you like it sweeter)

Instructions

Put the lavender flowers into a teapot/jug and cover with a litre of boiling water; leave this to steep for around 15 minutes.
Strain the flowers and then add the honey to the lavender water. I use 2 tbsp; you may like it sweeter
Add the juice of 2 lemons
Leave to cool in the fridge
Dilute it with still or sparkling water, with around 1/3 of the lemonade to 2/3 water
It will keep in the fridge for several days.

Lavender salve

I find this a soothing salve to use; it is great for dry skin, but it also feels so nurturing as it is gentle and smells amazing.

You will need

Dried lavender flowers (enough to fill 1/2 a jam jar)
Sweet almond oil or sunflower oil
Beeswax (pellets are easier to melt down)
Empty pots (I use old moisturiser pots)
Lavender essential oil

First, you need to make lavender oil

Fill a jam jar halfway with dried lavender flowers
Fill the jar almost to the top with a base oil. I use sweet almond oil or sunflower oil
Leave this in a dark place for around 3–4 weeks
Then strain the oil and put it back in the jar (with a label!)

For the salve

Use 50 ml of the lavender oil
14 g of beeswax or vegan equivalent
25 drops of lavender essential oil

Instructions

Put the lavender oil that you made earlier and the wax into a jug or bowl. Put this into a saucepan of boiling water (you're making a double boiler, as if you were melting chocolate). Gently heat on the stove.
Once the beeswax has melted, take it off the heat, let it cool for a few minutes, then add around 25 drops of lavender essential oil.
Pour into the tubs and allow to cool and set.

Cold-water swimming

For me, this is the best way to destress; it always works. I started cold-water swimming about 10 years ago, and the last seven or so years, I have been doing it all year round. This year, I have managed to cold-water swim at least once a week every week since last October (I am now in mid-August writing this). There is a growing body of research to show how cold-water swimming can be good for our mental health and stress levels. I will explore this more in the chapter on exercise. Last year, while writing my previous book and in the middle of an extremely difficult term at work, I found a lump in my breast. On the day of my appointment at the breast clinic, I went to the brook that runs through the farm where my husband's workshop is based and stood in the cold water for five minutes. I didn't have time to swim, but I knew the cold water was what I needed to balance me, nurture me, calm and soothe me. It felt so good, I remember walking out thinking ok, I am now ready to hear what this is. Thankfully, it was only a cyst, but each time I am back in that water space, I remember how it provided me with the moment of calm I needed.

Yoga and mindfulness

Both yoga and mindfulness are growing in popularity as a way of helping to deal with stress. Mindfulness is a technique which helps us to be fully present and in the moment without judging how we are feeling. With mindfulness, we often think of sitting and doing a meditation, but we can also do physically active meditations, such as walking or running. There is a growing number of apps which have meditations you can use. Some of my favourite apps are Smiling Mind (this is free) and Buddhify (this has a one-off charge). You can also do an eight-week mindfulness course. Most of these use Mark Williams and Danny Penman's course from their book, Mindfulness: A practical guide to finding peace in a frantic world (2011), but you can also find meditations from their book to use at home on their website, Frantic World. One thing to be aware of with mindfulness is that for some people who have experienced trauma, doing a mindfulness meditation can be triggering.

However, yoga does not seem to be triggering for people in the way that mindfulness sometimes can. Mindfulness is used within yoga, but yoga is also about moving. There are many different types of yoga that you can choose from. There has been a lot of research showing the impact of yoga on lowering stress and improving mood. You can go to organised classes, but there are also many online lessons for free. I particularly like Yoga with Adriene. I tend to dip in and out of yoga and mindfulness; they are practices I always return to when I can feel my stress levels rising.

Did you know?

Regularly practising yoga can help to reduce inflammation in the blood, and it can help protect your joints.

A breathing technique to try

Both mindfulness and yoga use breathing exercises. A very simple exercise you can do is 7/11 breathing. If you can feel yourself becoming very stressed and agitated, this simple technique helps to slow your heart rate.

Sit or stand comfortably
Take a breath in through your nose, counting to seven

Breathe out through your mouth, counting to 11
And repeat a few times
If you find the 7/11 too hard, try 5/7 instead
An alternative to this that I use a lot with children is bubble breathing.
1 pot of bubbles
Dip the wand into the bubble mixture
Take a deep breath
Blow slowly through the bubble wand
Getting children to do this can help them to find some calm, but if they find this too hard in that moment, you could blow the bubbles. Blowing the bubbles will bring you some calm and help to regulate yourself, which will then help to co-regulate the child.

Engaging in something joyful

I think this can be such a great stress reliver when we engage in a practice that brings us moments of joy. It might be through spending time with others that you love, the glimmers of joy through nature or maybe the joy you experience through exercise. Sometimes it can be helpful to have a reminder of what brings us joy. On my laptop, I have a photo page to remind me. I particularly call on this in moments in the winter when it feels gloomy, and I am feeling low; it reminds me of the practices I can do that may bring me some joy.

For this book, I have spoken with a variety of early years and educational people on what helps them with dealing with stress. Below are some of their thoughts; other examples will be shared throughout the book.

Kerry is an early years lecturer and author

Time alone. *I have very little social battery both offline and online. As I have gotten older, I know what brings me energy and what drains me, and I have become quite uncompromising about this. I am direct about what I can offer in terms of my time and engagement.*

Baths. *I take baths as much as I can. I am not sure why, but just having a bath makes me feel safe.*

Ignoring demands. *I detest living in a world where we are constantly bombarded with demands. Like any human right now, I use social media and tech too much, but I am also good at switching everything off, and ignoring everyone.*

Alistair is an early years trainer, consultant and author

Exercise. *I use exercise to help with stress. Just getting out from behind my laptop and into the fresh air makes a huge difference for me.*

Emily is a childminder

Being planned and organised. *I like to prep the evening before, so I know where everything is and enjoy the time with the children.*

Jamel is an early years trainer, consultant and author

What helps relieve my stress is doing things I enjoy: reading, being creative and watching cartoons. Going on walks or riding my bike also helps to lower my stress. These things also bring me joy, but additionally, being with my family, helping others and seeing them thrive is what brings me joy and happiness. Seeing how many lives I've touched and people enjoying and connecting with my books also makes me happy.

Emma is a Steiner, an early years worker

Something I struggle with is letting go of stressful situations in my day, and I constantly rerun them in my mind. Making sure I get out for a walk in nature every evening really does help to reset my mind and help me move on mentally.

Sarah is a Forest School leader

I have attended therapy sessions in the past to help me talk through complex situations, and I think everyone would benefit from talking therapy. I'm very lucky that my husband is very supportive and has been in my life for 30 years. Most important for me is that I acknowledge my feelings and take action if I become aware of the starting signs of toxic stress.

Aaron is an early years lecturer and writer

When stress builds, I find talking it through with someone I trust really helps. I also lean on journaling; writing down what's on my mind can take the weight off.

Conclusion

Being aware of how we respond to stress and what helps us is crucial for helping us to deal with it. Although, of course, it is not just the knowing but the action we take. I found the idea of having a menu of daily practices to release stress so helpful; it helped me feel proactive. I think it is great that we talk about stress more openly, but I hope this chapter has given you a few thoughts about recognising stress and maybe some ideas for actions you might be able to take.

Ideas on how to incorporate this into early years practice and at home

At the end of each chapter, I am going to add a short section on how we can incorporate some of these ideas into our early years practice, but you might also like to incorporate them into family life too, with your children or grandchildren or as part of your local community

- Have some hand cream in your room. This is great for use with both children and staff.
- Have a pot of bubbles on the side to use for bubble breathing, for both staff and children.
- Have an awe and wonder shelf: add natural things you and the children have found, such as leaves, shells and flowers. It can be added to and changed.
- Use yoga or mindfulness: Cosmic Kids on YouTube has both yoga and mindfulness practices you can use at home or in a setting with children. Using Cosmic Kids mindfulness can be great before bedtime.
- Have a go-to story book or rhyme book you can look at with the children that regularly makes you all laugh. Talk to the children about how laughter can help us feel less stressed.

The final part of each chapter is going to offer some practical things you can do, linked to different lengths of time.

If you have

If you have 2 minutes, do a hand massage with hand cream, paying attention to be slow and intentional.

If you had 10 minutes, you could try sitting outside with a hot drink, or if you don't have an outside space, sit by an open window. See if you can see anything that captures your wonder.

If you had 20 minutes, you could have a conversation with a friend or family member, maybe FaceTime them, ring them or sit and share a coffee with them.

If you had 40 minutes, you could do some exercise, maybe go for a walk or a run, or do an online exercise class or yoga.

References

Brené Brown interviews the Nagoski sisters: https://brenebrown.com/podcast/brene-with-emily-and-amelia-nagoski-on-burnout-and-how-to-complete-the-stress-cycle/

Buddhify app: https://buddhify.com/

Cosmic Kids: www.youtube.com/c/CosmicKidsYoga

Chaterjess, R. (2018). *The stress solution*, London: Penguin

Frantic World: https://franticworld.com/free-meditations-from-mindfulness/

Kirsten Neff: https://self-compassion.org/what-is-self-compassion/

Leibowitz, K. (2025). *How to winter*, London: Bluebird

Mainstone-Cotton, S. (2021). *Supporting children with social, emotional and mental health needs in the early years*, Oxford: Routledge

Mainstone-Cotton, S. and Cooke, S. (2025). *Help what do I do now?* Oxford: Routledge

Nagoski, E. and A. (2020). *Burnout*, London: Penguin

Neff, K. (2015). *Self-compassion*, New York: Harper Collins

Neurolaunch: https://neurolaunch.com/does-crying-release-cortisol/

Stress: https://www.mind.org.uk/information-support/types-of-mental-health-problems/stress/signs-and-symptoms-of-stress/

Smith, J. (2022). *Why has nobody told me this before?* London: Penguin
Smiling Mind app: https://www.smilingmind.com.au/smiling-mind-app/
Lavender salve: https://thenerdyfarmwife.com/lavender-salve-recipe-with-printable-labels/
Lavender lemonade: https://www.growforagecookferment.com/lavender-lemonade/
Williams, M. and Penman, D. (2011). *Mindfulness: A practical guide to finding peace in a frantic world,* London: Piatkus
Yoga: https://yogawithadriene.com/

2 Nature

I think this is my favourite chapter and subject. Over the years, I have learnt how being outside in nature always brings me a boost, whether by calming me, helping me process information or simply filling me with absolute joy and delight. For many of us, being able to walk during the COVID lockdowns was an essential boost to our wellbeing. For this book, I have been hearing from lots of different people in education and early years, and many of them have mentioned how being outside helps them. My aim with this chapter is to share some science around how and why nature helps us, but also to share the practical. I am going to share places to walk from across the UK that have been shared with me for this chapter. I am also going to share some thoughts on gardening, foraging and tree climbing, offering guidance, tips and recipes, and suggest ways based on the seasons of how you can engage in nature.

Mental health benefits

There has been increasing research into the benefits of being outside on our physical and mental health. From April 2021, there was a research project launched by the government in seven areas in the UK called green social prescribing (GSP), where GPs were referring people to take part in nature-based interventions such as gardening, walking and volunteering with conservation projects. One of the aims of the project was to improve mental health outcomes. The interim finding from the project showed positive improvements om mental health and wellbeing. The National Academy for

DOI: 10.4324/9781003717591-3

Social Prescribing wrote a briefing paper in 2022 about what the evidence is for nature, health and wellbeing. This suggests

Time spent in nature:

- Reduces blood pressure
- Reduces stress levels
- Reduces the risk of diabetes and obesity
- Increases wellbeing, including subjective wellbeing
- A decrease in PTSD and ADHD symptoms

This model is being rolled out with more GPs across the country engaging with the idea of green social prescribing. On doing this research, I found a great link to Intelligent Health, which has created a slideshow for GPs simply explaining the benefits of this idea (a link to this is in the references).

Green spaces

The term "green spaces" is often used in reference to supporting people's mental health. A green space can be a maintained or unmaintained area, and can vary between small and large parks, woodlands, nature reserves, allotment spaces, gardens or even graveyards (which can be a green space as they often a great place to find trees, plants and wildlife). Many new housing and business developments increasingly think about the green spaces being added to the new development; this isn't just in housing and business developments, but also in hospitals. In Bristol, their new hospital wing dedicated to heart surgery was developed a few years ago and has large windows throughout the building, bringing in a lot of light, and has large trees growing in the building. It is recognised that being around green spaces can boost mental and physical wellbeing and can help to aid recovery from illness, which is why hospitals are trying to have more green spaces around the building. Some research from Exeter University has found that spending 120 minutes in nature a week can benefit health and wellbeing. This doesn't need to be in one go; it can accumulate over the week.

Blue spaces

The other term you may have heard of is blue spaces. A page on the Environment Agency blog (2021) describes blue spaces as "outdoor environments – either natural or manmade – that prominently feature water and are accessible to people". Many people describe feeling a sense of calmness when they are near water. You don't have to be in the water to experience the positive effects, although some people feel drawn to being in it and find this a massive wellbeing boost. I'm definitely one of those people.

Moment for reflection

Just for a moment, think about your local green or blue spaces, where is it can you go to be in nature? It might be your garden or a local park; you may be lucky enough to live near water. How often do you go there?

Engaging with nature

In this section, I am going to explore ways we can engage with nature, with ideas from practitioners who engage in this regularly

Walking

Walking outside is available to most of us, unless your mobility is difficult, but hopefully, then you have someone/aids to support you. When I use the term walking, I am including using a wheelchair or similar. We don't need to go on long, rambling walks to get the benefits; even going for a short 10-minute walk will still benefit us. Michael Mosley did an episode of "Just one thing" (2021) on an early morning walk, and he suggests that getting out first thing in the morning can boost our wellbeing. The natural light first thing in the morning, particularly in the winter, can help people who experience seasonal affective disorder (SAD). Exposure to light in the morning can also help us sleep better later that day. If you're not a natural early riser, as long as you get outside within two hours of waking, it will still give you the same benefits.

The joy of living in the UK is that there are many amazing spaces to walk in, from local parks, woodlands, coasts, canals and riverbanks. The other joy of walking is that it is free, you can do it on your own or with others, you don't need special kit, although a raincoat is useful!

I am fortunate to live in a village on the outskirts of Bath, as mentioned in Chapter 1. We have a small community meadow which I often walk around if I don't have time for a longer walk. We also have a circular walk which takes about 50 minutes. The walk is through country lanes, past a farm with cows, along a brook where, occasionally, you can spot kingfishers, and along more country lanes with horses. I love doing this walk on an early morning if I am not swimming, and it's my local foraging walk (more on that below). It's the walk I do when I need to process information, work out a problem with work or think through a writing project. It's also the walk I do if I am feeling sad and anxious, and I always feel calmed and clearer after doing it.

There is sometimes an idea that walking is something that middle-class white people do; I would like to gently challenge this and suggest that walking should be for everyone. One of the groups that is challenging this idea is Black Girls Hike. They were set up in 2019 to create a safe space for black women to explore the outdoors. One of their aims is to diversify the countryside, letting people know it is a place for everyone to enjoy. Another group is the Walking Men in Lewisham, whose website describes their meetings as a "bi-weekly haven that merges invigorating walks and honest conversations, fostering growth and camaraderie among African Caribbean men". The BBC Countryfile online magazine has a really useful page linking to walking groups for people with disabilities across the UK. There is also a national organisation called Living Streets, whose website says "Something exciting is happening in communities up and down the country. People are getting together to reclaim their streets and neighbourhoods and improve them for walking". On the website, they have a list across the UK of different areas that are part of this. They are trying to make walking in our local area really accessible. While doing this research, I discovered there is a women's walking group in Bath, the nearest city to me, called Landgirls. If walking is something you are interested in, it might be worth seeing if there is a walking group in your area.

Many people walk daily as they have dogs, and find huge benefits to their wellbeing through dog walking. Below, Tamisn and Kerry talk about their experiences.

Tamsin: *We have a lovely cavapoo, Ruffle, and the best way that I help my mental health and also spend time in nature is walking him in a local country park or local woods. This not only keeps me fit and gives him a walk but also gives me some valuable time in a green space. On days when I can't get to the country park or woodland, I take him to a playing field so I still get my green fix and he gets to chase his ball.*

Kerry: *I also find walking my three chihuahuas with my husband an activity that is important. We go to the park most days for a 40-minute walk, and I find that is where I can shake off the residue of the day. I am an over-thinker and get into stuck states, and time to move at the end of a day is an important part of my repair.*

Barefoot walking

Have you ever tried barefoot walking? When I deliver wellbeing training in person, I often have participants do some barefoot walking in silence. It's fascinating seeing people's responses; some love the idea and are keen to participate, others look unconvinced and apprehensively try; and some just refuse, which is fine. But those who try it often say how much they enjoyed it, it made them slow down, notice in a way they may not usually do when walking.

People's experience of walking

Emma describes her experience of walking/wheeling:

I have always loved green spaces, finding peace when I'm under trees, on hillsides or wandering through lush valleys. Since becoming blind and then needing a wheelchair, I have found it almost impossible to get into these places and lose myself in the natural world. In fact, trying to get into nature became more frustrating than life-giving. Instead of trying to access the green, I turned to blue spaces, by the water, where access is often easier. Much as rivers and lakes are beautiful, it is the wide open skies of the coast which I now visit as much as I can. On the coast, I feel connected to the sea and sky, my mind becomes lighter and calmer, I can breathe deeper, and I feel less confined bodily and mentally. I feel a deep sense of relaxation and connection with the world when I wheelwalk, or even just sit by the sea; nowhere else do I feel so free. I find God in these wide blue spaces as the wind blows through my hair, the sea fills my senses, and my emotions can flow with joy or sorrow. I miss the sea viscerally if I don't get to it for several weeks; there is a deep yearning for natural connection that I know heals inner parts of me. By the sea, connected naturally, I can be comfortably me.

Jacki describes her experience:

It is one of the greatest gifts of this life of mine, walking. And knowing what walking can do for me. I have walked all over Ireland and Scotland, nights in bivvies, crawling on stormy ridges in the snow and summer days looking out to sea. I have walked in the High Atlas, the Himalayas, and the Simien mountains of Ethiopia, and I have had real adventures and remarkable experiences. Christmas Day in the Sahara, camping under the Milky Way after a meal of bread cooked in ash under the sand. Yet . . .

One of the things I value most is the regular walks, through a landscape or a cityscape, which changes in ways only I know and become the familiar touchstone. In Newcastle, the walk into university through Brandling Village; in Edinburgh, the restoration after shifts, up on Salisbury Crags, in Corsham, out to the Box Valley, barley, swifts, beautiful but never quite enough for me. Most of all, the Irish coast I grew up on, the shoreline laced with oyster catchers, seals out on the rocks, guillemots. I know every shell on that shore.

I live now between the Ochils and the start of the southern highlands. I can see Ben Vorlich, Ben Lawers, up towards the Cairngorms; all the spots on the horizon I thought I'd head to every Friday night, packing the tent, the stove, into the car. But no, I have stayed close to home, exploring what is in front of me and valuing that "on the doorstep" walking. I have again carved out a ritual in my walking that eases my soul and brings me back to myself, if not immediately, eventually. In the noticing of the endless shifts in the ground beneath me, the moss and lichen, the trees above me, cones dropping, leaves turning, the red squirrels scuttling, the deer in the early December mornings running through the snow in the still darkness. The paths made by deer and sheep, no human hand moulding them, and the shapes they have taken with many feet like mine weaving through.

And it is through this watching and observing that I have come to know where I live and to truly value how my own self knows what it needs to be well and to recover wellness. I always walk back to myself, but I often take myself further, explore my own horizons, reach to where I think I could take myself in my thinking, my learning, my actions. That's what is exciting. As I get older, that's where walks take me – to challenge myself to keep expanding, to not narrow in, to see more on this treasured little patch of earth and to understand it more deeply. In so doing, I learn to more fully be myself, to go with my moments of energy, to listen to the vulnerabilities, the limits, and to continue to put one foot in front of the other.

Sara describes one of her favourite places where she walks and wild swims:

I'm thinking of Rannerdale Knott, above Crummock Water.

I tend to walk up the back of it through the "secret" bluebell valley, where it is said the bluebells grow so well out in the open because they're fertilised by the blood of a thousand Roman soldiers, who were killed there by Celts. It's a slow, steady walk up the valley, and then you turn right up a steep little track, rocky but not technical. After 10 minutes, you pop out on the grassy slopes of Rannerdale and can either walk left or right. Go right as if you're walking on towards the tops, but actually, if you just cross straight ahead, you will reach the most beautiful viewing point. You can lie on the tufty grass and stare at the two lakes lying before you. Buttermere to your left and Crummock to your right. It is a walk best described as before 1 pm-ish so that the sun is either behind you or to your left – no silhouette of the mountains across the waters . . .

You can then either carry on up and down, with a few harder, more scrambly bits to the trig point. Then descend the same way you came up or down the end of the Knott, dropping towards Crummock. It's steep, rocky staircase, quite manageable unless you have bad knees! A Wainwright but very versatile and doable.

Moment for reflection

Just for a moment, think about your favourite walk. This might be a local one, or one you did with family and friends on holiday. Notice how it makes you feel when you think of it.

Did you know?

It requires 200 muscles in our body to take one step. That is why walking is considered a full-body exercise.

The joy of walking

For me, I often find going for a walk a joyful experience. I walk without headphones so that I can be more present with what is around me. I find this helps me notice more, both the sounds and also the sights on my walk. We regularly walked with our daughters; in all honesty, that wasn't always joyful! There were moments when their small legs were unhappy about climbing the local hills, or as stroppy teens, they were not keen. But overall, I have many wonderful memories of walking as a family. And there are still places we visit that have strong, precious memories for me of walks as a family

Walks to try

In researching this book, I have been asking people for recommendations of walks across the UK, and here they are. There is a link to each walk at the end of the chapter. I have tried to capture suggestions from across the UK, but I am aware I have missed many places, and I apologise for that.

Southwest

Alison recommends in Somerset Circular walk through Mells, ending through a medieval churchyard where Siegried Sassoon is buried

Nettie recommends the Somerset levels: Ham Wall (also a great place to watch starling murmurations in the winter)

Karen recommends in North Somerset: Sandpoint and Middle Hope circular coastal walk, near Weston Super Mare

Kieran recommends in Bath: Little Solsbury Hill (famous from Peter Gabriel's song, which I am listening to as I write this!)

Louie recommends in Bristol -Badocks woods (this is very accessible for wheelchairs; her daughter can use her electric wheelchair here easily)

Gemma recommends the Gloucester and Sharpness canal walk

Sharon recommends Wiltshire Shearwater Lake

Emma recommends Dorset Mudeford Quay to Avon beach. She does this in her wheelchair

Iain recommends Dartmoor, Devon: Buckland Beacon (he recarved some stones on here that have the Ten Commandments on them, which originated from 1928)

Karen recommends in South Cornwall: The Tinners Way walk, St Ives to St Just (I have done some of this walk, and it is stunning)

Naomi recommends in North Cornwall: Cawsand to Penlee Point

Southeast

Ann recommends a New Forest walk: Coppice of Linwood

Tessa recommends Richmond Park in London

Jenny recommends the London Capital Ring walk, which has 15 sections, each with a tube station near it

Will recommends in Essex: Dedham Constable country loops of Flatford to Dedham Vale

Summer recommends in Oxford: the university park behind St Catherine's college

East of England

Chris recommends in Cambridge: Wandlebury Country Park

Sharon recommends in Suffolk: Woodbridge circular walk

Graham recommends in Hertfordshire: Harcamlow Way, this is one long walk (141 miles) which can be done in small sections

East Midlands

Ailsa recommends in Derbyshire Nine Ladies Stone Circle walk

Tony recommends Leicestershire: The Outwoods (apparently has a nice tea stop!)

Kathy recommends Lincolnshire: The fens

West Midlands

Tim recommends Worcester: the Malvern Hills

Marie recommends Shropshire: Wyre Forest

Beckah recommends the Birmingham canal walk

Yorkshire and Humber

Amanda recommends Sheffield: Five Weirs Walk

Ruth recommends West Yorkshire: Ilkley Moor

Rachel recommends a walk in the Huddersfield area: Castle Hill walk

Marnie recommends a walk in York: Askham Bog

North West

Lois recommends Cheshire: Whitegate Way

Sara recommends Cumbria: Crummock Water (you can see a further description of this walk from Sara above)

Marnie recommends Lancashire: Pendle Hill walk. She says it has a cool monument and is drenched in folklore

Rosie recommends North Cumbria: Maryport to Grune Point

North East

Sonia recommends a walk on Lindisfarne: North Shore walk (add a swim on north beach for a perfect combination!)

Pete recommends the Housesteads: Steel Rigg circular walk, which is part of Hadrian's wall

Iain recommends walking in Kielder Forest

Wales

Sarah recommends the Brecon Beacons and having a dip in the waterfalls (I have done this many times and it's amazing!)

Claire recommends in mid-Wales: Tor Y Foel mountain

Sara recommends the Gower Coast: Three Cliffs Bay walk

Sonia recommends in Pembrokeshire: St Davids Head coastal walk

Scotland

Gayle recommends the Glasgow mural walk; this can be as long or short as you want. This is a city walk

Karen recommends the island of Orkney, the walk from Yesnaby to Stromness

Gayle recommends the Isle of Lewis: around the Butt of Lewis (I have done this walk and saw whales!)

Gayle recommends the Isle of Harris: Northton Machair and Temple

Lily recommends Edinburgh: the Arthur's Seat circular walk

Jackie recommends walks in the Ochil Hills, the southern highlands

Sonia recommends the Isle of Iona: walk to North Beach (North Beach is one of my favourite places to swim)

Foraging

I find one of the joys of walking is foraging alongside. I have picked blackberries since childhood and have strong memories of doing this with my nan in Wales, and I have carried on this tradition with my children. Around 15 years ago, I went on a study trip to a Danish nursery, which was situated on the edge of a woodland. During this visit, we all went for a walk, and I noticed the children eating what they found as they walked, but also the older children warning the younger children not to eat certain mushrooms. I was filled with awe at seeing these children. I loved how connected the children were to this space; they respected the land but also had the knowledge about what foods were ok and not ok to eat. I felt hugely challenged as I realised these young children had a lot more knowledge of what was edible than I did. I have since discovered through my eldest daughter living in Oslo that there is a rich shared knowledge and history of foraging in Scandinavian countries. In Oslo, if you go foraging for mushrooms in the autumn, they have information stations in the woods with volunteers sharing advice and identifying your finds for you. When I returned from the Danish trip, I decided to learn what was available to eat for free in my area. And since then, I have been a huge fan of foraging, and I am still learning what I can pick and what I can make. I think one of the benefits of foraging is that it forces you to slow down; you can't find the fruit/leaves/berries if you're walking past quickly. There is also something so satisfying about getting food for free! And then making it into something nourishing and nurturing.

We can often think that foraging is just for those who live in rural areas, but you can forage in towns and cities, if you know where to find the free food. My youngest daughter has recently moved to Oxford, and she discovered a foraging map of the city.

Jamel wrote about foraging in London with his son

Jamel on foraging

In the inner city of London, nature is all around us. We have huge parks and green spaces like Greenwich, Blackheath and Mountsfield Park, Lewisham Park, Ladywell Park and more.

Around the area we are blessed to have wild fruits, herbs and flowers. I often take my son out with me and pick lavender, sage or raspberries and blackberries. Which is fun because we can use our senses to find, smell, touch and taste each fruit we find.

Currently, while I am writing this section of the book, it's mid-September, and I am back in schools, meeting the children I am supporting this year. I know that as the term goes on, there will be many bugs and germs, so my current foraging is mostly focused on boosting my immune system. In the autumn section below, I share my elderberry liquor recipe. This is a great immune-boosting recipe. Autumn is, of course, a fantastic time to forage. I am going to share with you some ideas below of things you can forage throughout the year.

Foraging safety tips

Before I go any further, I need to highlight that we need to forage safely and sustainably. A few useful tips

- Do your research first; if in doubt, don't pick it. There are many useful books on foraging, the first one I bought after the Danish trip was *Food for free* by Richard Mabey (2012), it's a small pocket-sized book, and really useful. There are also some really useful apps. I use the app called Seek a lot; it identifies plant species and animals, and it is free. There is also an app called Foragers Log, which lets you log on to a map when you have found things, but also identifies plants (based on other postings).

- Start with something obvious that you can't get wrong. There might be an apple tree growing in your local park that has sprouted up from someone discarding a pip. Or there might be blackberries along the canal where you live. As mentioned above, don't pick something and eat it unless you are sure you know it is edible. There have been awful cases of people poisoning themselves.
- Only pick what you will use; don't pick all the leaves/berries on a plant. Don't pull up the bulbs, e.g., with wild garlic.
- Be aware of the pollution around. If picking blackberries, it's best to avoid busy road sides as they will have so much car fumes on them. Don't pick in areas where they have been sprayed with chemicals; some councils do this in parks.
- Minimise damage to the area you are picking from. You can do this by sticking to paths, trying not to trample over plants and not breaking branches.

For more guidance notes on foraging, look at the Woodland Post pages on foraging.

Moment for reflection

Do you have a memory of foraging? This may have been as a child or more recently.

Foraging through the year

Below are some of my suggestions for what you can pick through the seasons. If you are making things to keep in glass bottles or jars, you need to sterilise them first. This is very simple to do:

Wash glass bottles and jars in warm, soapy water

Then put them in the oven on a low heat until they are dry

Winter

Wild garlic is one of the first plants to appear at the start of the year that we can forage. In my area, you can find the leaves from around mid-February. You will know wild garlic from its distinctive smell of garlic, although you do need to be careful, as there is another leaf which looks similar but is poisonous, and that leaf does not smell of garlic. The trick is to pick the leaves individually, not in a handful; that way, you know you're getting the garlic leaf from the smell. Further north in the country, it appears slightly later. Wild garlic is available for a few months. You can eat the leaves and the flowers, which appear slightly later than the leaves. My favourite recipes are wild garlic pesto and wild garlic soda bread. A link to finding wild garlic is in the references. Similar to wild garlic is three-cornered leek, it looks a bit like grass or chives but it has triangular stems and smells of onions. So far, I haven't found this plant in my area, but I regularly find it in coastal areas in Cornwall. This can bc found from January. I have put a link in the reference about identifying this plant.

Did you know?

Eating wild garlic may help to reduce blood cholesterol and lower blood pressure (similar to garlic)

Wild garlic soda bread

Ingredients

400 g plain flour
1teaspoon salt
1 1/2 tsp of bicarbonate of soda
1 handful of wild garlic, washed and cut up small
300 ml milk
1/2 lemon juiced (or 2 tsp of bottled lemon juice)

Instructions

Pre heat the oven to 180C/350F/Gas 4.
Grease a bread tin.
Put the lemon juice into the milk and stir, put to one side while weighing other ingredients (the milk will look like it is curdling, that is correct!).
Weigh and sieve the flour, salt and bicarbonate of soda.
Make a well in the middle of the flour and pour in the milk mixture and wild garlic.
Mix with a wooden spoon; it will be sticky. If you think it is too sticky, add a little more flour.
You don't need to knead soda bread; the trick is to handle it as little as possible.
Add to your tin and score the top of the loaf.
Bake for 40 minutes.
When it is baked, it will sound hollow when tapped underneath.

Wild garlic pesto

Ingredients

4–6 handfuls of wild garlic
50 g of Parmesan cheese (or other hard cheese)
50 g of pine nuts (or other nuts, walnuts also work well)
A glug of olive oil
A small amount of lemon juice

Instructions

Put all the ingredients into a blender and blend them together.
This is one of those recipes you need to taste as you go along, you may find it needs more oil, cheese or lemon juice.
You want it to be a lovely green colour and smooth texture.
Put into a jar and will keep in the fridge for around a week.
This is great added to pasta or mashed potatoes.

Nettles, another plant that is easy to identify. If you have a garden, you will see them appearing around March or April. The best time to pick the nettle

leaves is when they are young. Nettles are full of iron and vitamins A and D. Pick them using gardening gloves. You can use them in a nettle tea by pouring boiling water over the leaves (this takes the sting out of them), or my favourite is to make nettle and wild garlic soup. I did once make a nettle cordial, but my family thought it was disgusting!

Nettle and wild garlic soup

Ingredients

3 handfuls of wild garlic
6 handfuls of nettle leaves
1 celeriac
1 potato
1 leek
1 onion
1 litre of vegetable stock

Instructions

Fry the onion and leek
Peel and chop the potato and celeriac, sweat these with the onion and leek for around 5 minutes.
Pour in the stock and simmer until the potatoes and celeriac are almost cooked
Add the nettles and wild garlic for a few minutes until they have wilted
Blend together.
This goes well with the sourdough recipe above.

Spring

Elderflowers-grow in hedgerows, on verges, in parks and gardens. For me elderflowers are indicative of spring. The flowers are creamy white in colour, and grow in clusters, and again they have a distinctive floral smell. They usually appear in May. There is a link in the references to the BBC Countryfile program on how to identify them. My favourite recipes are elderflower cordial and elderflower lemon curd; the lemon curd feels like the taste of spring/early summer, I love that recipe. Make sure you leave some flowers on the tree as these will later grow into elderberries.

Elderflower cordial recipe

Ingredients

25 elderflower heads
Grated zest of 3 lemons and their juice
400 g of sugar
1 heaped teaspoon of citric acid (this helps to keep it for longer, but it's not essential)

Instructions

Gently shake the flower heads to dislodge any bugs.
Put the flowers in a bowl with lemon zest.
Pour 1.5 litres of water over the flowers and leave overnight to infuse.
Drain the liquid; you can use a jelly bag or a sieve.
Pour the liquid into the saucepan.
Add the sugar, lemon juice and sugar.
Simmer gently until the sugar has dissolved.
Pour into sterilised bottles.
Be sure to dilute it with water before drinking it!

Elderflower lemon curd

Ingredients

200 g castor sugar
2 lemons juiced and zest
55 g unsalted butter
7 elderflower heads
2 eggs beaten

Instructions

Rinse the flower heads and spin in a salad spinner to dry them remove insects.
Put the sugar, lemon juice, zest and butter in a pan.

Cut the flowers off the stalks and add them to the mixture in the pan.
Put the pan on a low heat and stir until the sugar has dissolved, but don't let it simmer.
Remove the pan from the heat and leave the elderflowers to steep for 10 minutes.
Sieve the contents of the pan to remove the flower heads.
Put the mixture back in the pan and add the beaten eggs.
Keep whisking the mixture.
When the curd starts to boil, keep whisking and cook for another minute or two.
If it looks slightly lumpy, strain through a sieve.
Pour into sterilised jars.
This will keep for a few weeks in the fridge. It tastes amazing on crumpets and toast and in a cake.

Wild honeysuckle flowers grow as a climbing plant in hedgerows and at the edge of woodlands. They taste incredibly sweet. You can pick the flowers and add them to water and prosecco, or you can add them to jam and jellies. You don't need many. As a family, we always pick some when we do the coastal walk from Carbis Bay to St Ives in Cornwall (a popular walk when we holiday there) and eat them as we walk. The Woodland Trust has a web page about identifying these flowers.

Summer

Wild fruits: during the summer months, you can find wild fruits such as wild strawberries, wild raspberries, red currants and early blackberries. But this is about knowing your area; where I live, there are not many of these to be found, but we can find blackberries growing along the canal from the beginning of August.

Crab apples are very small apples, often red or pink in colour. You can pick them in August. They are very sour and not eating apples, but they are really high in pectin and are great for using in jams and jellies with other fruit. I made a crab apple jelly this year, and the colour was a beautiful pink. You find these in hedgerows, fields and on the edge of woodland. The Woodland Trust has a web page about identifying crab apples.

Crab apple jelly

Ingredients

1 kg of crab apples
600 g granulated sugar

Instructions

Remove the stalks and chop the apples (you can use the whole fruit).
Place in a saucepan with 1.25 litres of water.
Slowly simmer until the apples are soft.
Strain overnight or for a few hours through a sieve or jelly bag.
Measure the liquid, and for each litre of liquid, add 600g of granulated sugar, and then bring to the boil until it is set (around 10 minutes). You know it is set when you add a teaspoon of liquid to a cold plate and it starts to set.
Pour into jars.
This can be kept in a dark place up to a year.

Autumn

Blackberries are an easy plant to find and identify in the autumn (although I discovered from my sister they don't grow in Orkney). As mentioned, in some areas you can find them in the summer. Blackberries are a perfect plant to get children started with foraging. My favourite recipes are blackberry and pistachio salad, blackberry cordial, and blackberry curd (use the elderflower curd recipe above but replace the elderflower with 200 g of blackberries). Of course, a blackberry and apple crumble is also wonderful.

Blackberry and nut salad

Ingredients

200 g blackberries
A few handfuls of rocket or other salad leaves

A few handfuls of pistachios or walnuts
1 block of feta cheese

Dressing

1 tbsp of grainy mustard
1 tbsp of honey
1 tbsp of vinegar (white or cider vinegar)
1 tbsp of olive oil
Splash of lemon juice

Instructions

Chop the cheese into small chunks.
Mix with the rocket, blackberry and pistachios.
Mix the dressing ingredients and pour the dressing over the salad.

Blackberry cordial

Ingredients

750 g of Blackberries
Enough cold water to cover them
1 small cinnamon stick
1 tsp of lemon juice
150 g of sugar

Instructions

Wash the blackberries and put them in a pan.
Pour over water, enough to just cover them.
Boil until the blackberries burst.
Mash the blackberries with a potato masher.
Strain through a sieve.
Put the blackberry juice, sugar, lemon juice, and cinnamon in a pan and boil for around 10 minutes.
Pour into a sterilised bottle.
I use the leftover fruit mixture, mixed with apple, to make a crumble.

Sweet chestnuts are quite easy to identify, although you need to make sure you don't mix these up with horse chestnuts (conkers); once you know they do look different. Sweet chestnuts are great to collect with children and then roast them on a fire or in the oven. You will mostly find them in parks or woodland around September/October. There is a link to identifying these at the end of this chapter from the Woodland Trust.

Rosehips are easy to spot; you find them in hedgerows. They are ready for picking in the autumn. Some sites say to pick after the first frosts, but I pick them earlier, and they still taste great. I make a rosehip syrup, and I take it as a shot when I feel rundown. Rosehips are high in vitamins A, B, C, E and K. The Canal River Trust website has a useful page about identifying rosehips. They do have tiny hairs in them (they used to be used in itching powder), so you need to strain them well.

Did you know?

Rosehips have 20 times more vitamin C than an orange! During World War 2, when oranges were hard to buy, people made rosehip syrup to ward off scurvy.

Rosehip syrup

500 g of rosehips
250 g of granulated sugar
750 ml water

Instructions

Wash the rosehips.
Put the rosehips into a blender or food processor to roughly chop them.
Put them into a saucepan and add 750 ml of water.
Bring to the boil and then simmer for around 20 minutes.
Strain the mixture through a double layer of muslin in a sieve (allow it around 30–45 minutes to strain).

Compost the mixture from the sieve, rinse the muslin and sieve and then re-strain the liquid one final time.
Put the liquid back in the pan with 125 g of sugar for every 250 ml of liquid.
Heat slowly until the sugar has dissolved.
Pour into sterilised bottles.
Keep in the fridge for around three months.

Elderberries: you will find these in the same location as the elderflowers (as long as you didn't pick all the elderflowers!). They are high in vitamin C and high in antioxidants, both of which are good for helping you fight off colds. You cannot eat them raw as they taste bitter and are mildly poisonous! But you can cook with them. You can find them from the end of August through to October. Every year, I make elderberry liquor; it's a recipe I have adapted over the years and in our family we take it at the first sign of a cold coming on. This year has been a great year for fruits, and I have made masses of liquor, sharing among family and friends, and I always make a batch for each member of our team. The BBC Good Food website has a useful page on elderberries.

Elderberry liquor

Ingredients

250 g of apples
400 g of elderberries
300 g sugar
200 g honey
2 tsp of chilli flakes
5 cm of ginger grated
300 ml of water
Juice of 1 lemon
100 ml of brandy (or whisky/rum is fine)

Instructions

Roughly chop the apples; use all of the apples.
Put them in a pan with all the other ingredients, apart from the alcohol.

> Simmer gently for around 15 minutes.
> Take off the heat and strain through a sieve.
> Add the alcohol and pour into sterilised bottles.

These are just a few easy finds for you to forage. You will notice I haven't listed any mushrooms. This is because I don't trust myself to identify these properly, so I tend to stay clear of foraging for fungi!

I think introducing children to safe foraging is a joyful activity: the process of picking the blackberries, persuading the children not to eat everything they find, and then bringing them home, making a crumble and eating it together is full of joy.

Gardening

I mentioned at the start of this chapter the idea of social prescribing, where GPs are referring people to take part in nature-based activities and how gardening is one of those. The Royal Horticultural Society (RHS) suggests that research they did showed that people who gardened regularly had high wellbeing scores and lower stress scores. It also suggests that gardening for half an hour burns off similar calories to playing badminton or volleyball. The RHS has an excellent section on their website exploring the benefits of gardening for health and wellbeing, tips on getting started and things to grow, as well as people's stories of how gardening has supported them.

I have a garden, and I find it to be a significant boost to my mental health. I try to grow vegetables, herbs, fruit and flowers, year on year; it is massively hit-and-miss about what grows and what doesn't! My gardening is quite wild and chaotic, but I love it. I think what I love about it is how I can get completely caught up in the moment of gardening. I find it a really helpful mindful practice, similar to cold water swimming, in that when I am gardening, I am often totally engaged and engrossed in what I am doing, and I don't think about other things.

You don't need to have your own garden; you can still grow things from a windowsill inside or a window box outside. Below, I am going to share a few ideas of things you could plant

Did you know?

Gardening can burn up to 300 calories an hour!

Bulbs

I love growing bulbs; plant them once, and they will come back year after year. They are cheap to buy, and you can now buy many of them in supermarkets. I mainly think of planting bulbs in the autumn, ready to flower in the spring. I find the act of planting bulbs in the autumn an act of hope. As the days are drawing in, it's getting colder, and plants are dying, so planting bulbs is a sign to remind me that there will be new growth again, more colour and lighter days ahead. You can plant bulbs inside; you don't need an outside space for this, and if you plant them in the autumn, some will be ready around Christmas and early January. You can also plant bulbs in the spring for summer flowering, although these are usually larger and ones you generally grow outside.

Bulbs are so easy to grow with children. I grow them in the autumn every year with the children I support, for them to take home. In the nurseries I work with, we do lasagne planting (see below) to grow in the nursery garden. My youngest daughter has just left home to start a new job in Oxford, and I have set her up with bulbs to plant. It's definitely an activity to share with others.

Bulbs you could plant in the autumn to appear in spring are:

Daffodils
Hyacinth
Crocus
Tulip
Grape hyacinth
Iris

Bulbs you can plant in spring for the summer

Dhalias
Begonias

Lilies
Gladioli
Iris

Below are some tips and suggestions on planting bulbs

Hyacyinths

These are such bold flowers, and I love their smell; they come in a wide variety of colours from whites, purples, pinks, reds, blues and yellows. If you grow them in a pot inside and you have an outside space, once they have died, plant the bulb outside, and they will keep coming back year after year. You can grow these easily inside and outside.

To plant in a pot for growing inside

Find a pot with holes in the bottom.

Fill your pot with compost.

Put a bulb in the pot on top of the compost (normally, bulbs you cover with compost, but planting these for inside, you plant them on top.)

Water them lightly.

Cover the pot with newspaper or similar and put it in a dark place for around 10 weeks. When a green shoot appears, bring it into a sunny spot.

To plant in water

You can grow hyacinths in water in a glass jar. This is a lovely activity to do with children, but I love doing it too! You can use any hyacinth bulb for this, but for most bulbs, you need to keep them chilled in a fridge for weeks, or you can buy them prepared. My local garden nursery sells hyacinth bulbs individually at 50p each or 60p for prepared bulbs. Last weekend, I bought 10 of the unprepared ones to grow in pots inside. Some of these I will give as presents, and the two prepared ones to grow in water to have at home.

You need a glass vase which has a narrow neck/an hourglass neck. You can buy them for planting bulbs or use a narrow glass jar.

Fill the jar to just below the point where the bulb sits; the bulb does not want to sit in water, but the water reaches up to the bulb.

Place the pot in a dark place.

Once there are a lot of roots, and you have a green shoot at the top of the bulb, bring it out of the dark and put it in a light spot.

Growing outside

You can plant them in pots outside or into a bed.

Find a sunny spot.

Plant them around 10 cm deep and 8 cm apart.

They will flower around March–April

For more information on growing hyacinths, the Gardeners' World website has a useful page with information.

Lasagne bulb planting

This might sound bizarre, but it's a useful way to grow several different varieties of bulbs in one pot. The idea is to layer the bulbs (as you would in making a lasagne!).

The idea is to plant the bulbs that will flower first on the top layer.

Have a pot with holes in the bottom (one big enough to fit in layers of bulbs).

Put some soil into the bottom of the pot (some pots recommend putting some stones or broken crockery covering the hole to help with drainage. I rarely do this, and it is usually fine!).

The first bulbs you put in are the ones that will flower last.

Cover these with compost.

Plant your next layer of bulbs.

Cover these with compost.

Plant your final layer of bulbs and cover these.

A combination I often plant is:

Bottom layer: tulip
Second layer: narcissus
Top layer: grape hyacinths

Plant these in the autumn, outside. On top of the soil, you could plant some wintering flowers such as winter pansies, violas or cyclamens. These will flower through the winter until your bulbs begin to appear.

For more tips on lasagne bulb planting, there is a website called Growing Family, which gives more information.

Moment for reflection

In the spring, do you know spots where you live where you can see snowdrops or daffodils growing? In Bath, daffodils can be found along the verges of many of the main roads; it's so joyful spotting these.

Growing food

There is something incredibly satisfying about growing your own food. Food you have grown always seems to taste better. You don't have to have a garden to grow your own food; you can grow food from pots on a balcony, patio or outdoor window sill. You can also grow some food inside. Growing your own food is a simple way to engage with nature. Below are some suggestions on growing food:

Herbs

Herbs are great for growing. You can use herbs in cooking, baking and making tea (fresh mint tea is amazing). Some herbs are hard to start from seed, although basil and coriander grow quite easily from seed. You may find that the herb plants you buy in the supermarket die quite quickly, but don't take that as an indication of not being able to grow herbs. They are packed into the tubs so tightly that they are not one plant but several plants. However, buying a supermarket herb can be a cheaper way to grow herbs. Below are some tips on what you can do:

How to split a herb plant

Take a supermarket pot of coriander/basil/mint/ thyme/parsley/tarragon.

Take the plant out of the pot.

Use your fingers to gently separate into several plants; try not to break the roots.

Plant these separate plants into small pots with compost and water them.

Put them on a windowsill or keep them outside if there is no chance of a frost.

Potatoes

I have a garden, but I now grow all my potatoes in tubs. Growing potatoes in the ground takes up quite a lot of space, whereas growing them in a tub enables me to grow them alongside other plants in the garden. You can buy seed potatoes from a garden centre, or sometimes supermarkets sell them in the spring. But you can grow potatoes from any old ones you have at home. If you have a potato that has started to send out shoots, you can plant it!

Growing potatoes

Find a large pot with holes in the bottom, or you can use a thick plastic bag, and put a few holes in the bottom.

Fill around 10 cm (4 inches) with peat-free compost.

Place 3 potatoes on the top of the compost, then cover them with another 10 cm (4 inches) of compost.

Put this in a sunny spot, and water it weekly if it hasn't rained.

As green shoots start to appear, cover these up with more compost.

Keep repeating this until the compost is at the top of the pot.

Once flowers appear, you can dig up the potatoes for new potatoes, or you can leave them until the foliage has died down, and the potatoes will be a bit bigger. Potatoes grown in a pot will be smaller to those grown in the ground.

Tomatoes

I think tomatoes are one of the easiest plants to grow from seed. You can buy a pack of seeds from a garden centre or supermarket for around £3. You can grow them from seed on a sunny windowsill from January. Tomatoes like warmth and light, and they do grow better in a greenhouse or conservatory, but you can grow them outside in a sheltered spot. Years ago, I had a friend who grew tomatoes in the small glass porch at the front of his rented house; they grew into huge vines with a great crop of tomatoes, and the smell was amazing as you walked into the tiny porch through the summer!

Growing tomatoes

Put around 3 cm (1 ¼ inches) of compost into a small container – I often use a grape container. Make sure it has drainage holes in it.

Sprinkle the seeds on top and lightly cover with more compost.

Keep them watered, but don't drown them!

After around a week, you will see some seedlings appear.

When the plants have grown their second set of seeds, you can carefully lift them and put them into their own individual pots with compost. I often use old yoghurt pots or similar.

They need to stay inside until the risk of frost has passed.

Once they are about 15 cm high (6 inches), plant them into the ground, or a bigger pot or a growbag (you can buy tomato plant grow bags).

If you're growing them outside, it is worth having them in a sheltered spot or against a warm wall. You will also need a stick to tie them against as they get taller. Keep watering them and pick them once they have ripened.

For more ideas on growing your food, I recommend the book by Simon Akeroyd, *Grow your own groceries* (2025), which is excellent, and he is on Instagram as simonakeroydgardenwriter

Growing flowers

Growing flowers brings me joy. I am going to suggest a few easy ones that can be grown in pots or in the ground.

Nasturtium: these have bold flowers in oranges, reds and yellows, and they are easy to grow. You can buy a packet of seeds in the supermarket or garden centre. They are large, knobbly seeds, which make them particularly good for children to grow, as they are easy to pick up and plant, and they grow quickly. You can plant them from March to May, and they flower from June to the first frosts. You can grow them in the ground where you want them to flower, in pots or hanging baskets. Plant them around 9 cm in the soil. I have them all over my garden, in the veg patch, herb patch and in hanging baskets. The joy with nasturtiums is that they look great, and you can eat the flowers and leaves in salads. The flowers taste slightly peppery. Once they have died over, you will get more seeds, so pick these, dry them out and keep them for the next year.

Calendula: these are part of the marigold family, but they look different and smell different to French marigolds (I don't like the smell of French marigolds, but I love the smell of calendula). They are traditionally an old cottage garden flower. They are orange and yellow. You can buy the seeds in supermarkets or garden centres. These are another flower that is very easy to grow, and again, you can grow these in pots and in the ground. Calendula is a great flower for pollinators; it will attract bees and butterflies. You plant them in March–May, and they flower from June to the first frosts. You can put the leaves in salads and drinks; you can also dry the leaves and use them in tea or use them in balm making. I grow a lot of calendula; it self-seeds, and I have them all over the garden. I dry them and use them in soap making and balm making. I also cut them and put them around my house; it is such a cheerful flower.

Sunflower: such a familiar flower and wonderful to grow, I love how bold and cheerful sunflowers are. Again, you buy these seeds in supermarkets and garden centres. You can plant these in the ground or in pots from April–May, and they will flower from July onwards. We mostly think of sunflowers being very tall, but you can get smaller ones now, which are easier to grow in a pot. I grow sunflowers every year with the children I work with, and we have conversations over the weeks about how big their sunflowers are growing. We have done sunflower-growing competitions as a family and as a team. Although in the team, it turned out someone sent false photos to say theirs was the tallest!

If you want further tips on growing flowers, Gardeners' World magazine online is an excellent free resource.

Did you know?

It can take up to 10,000 caterpillars to rear a brood of blue tits! By planting sunflowers, nasturtium and calendula, you will be attracting butterflies and helping your local birds!

Indoor plants

An alternative to growing things outside is having some indoor plants. It is thought that growing plants indoors can help to alleviate stress and anxiety and reduce blood pressure, in the way that being outside among plants is a big benefit, living with plants can also benefit us. Having plants indoors can also help to absorb air pollutants.

If you have a friend with a spider plant or aloe vera, ask them if you can have a baby plant. Spider plants and aloe veras are always producing baby plants, which are perfect for sharing. They are also plants that thrive on neglect so they are quite easy to grow. I recently gifted a spider plant to each of the trainee early years teachers I was teaching. I am not sure that was what they were expecting from their guest lecturer. My suggestion was that they could hopefully keep it alive until they get their first jobs, and then have it in their classrooms.

Some suggestions of plants to grow inside that are relatively easy to grow are:

Peace lily
Spider plant
Aloe vera (the juice in these is great to use if you burn yourself)
Chinese money plant
Snake plant
Lucky plant, sometimes called Jade plant

The key to growing plants inside is to water them enough (not too much) and find the right spot for them to grow with enough light. In my experience, this can be trial and error, and sometimes you need to move your plants to different rooms until you find the right spot.

For more information on growing indoor plants, the RHS has a useful page on their website.

Bird spotting

You might think of bird spotting as being a bit specialist, or it might make you think of middle-aged men in camouflage and big cameras. Bird spotting is not just for the obsessive enthusiasts; we can all engage in a bit of bird spotting, and I would like to suggest it can be joyful. In the UK, we are so fortunate to have a wide range of native birds and many migrating visitors. Yes, there is a problem with the population decline of some birds, but there is good news, too; some birds are doing well. In the area I live in, since COVID, red kites have appeared. They are a magnificent bird to see, and it still brings me joy every time I see them. Watching birds is free; we can all do it wherever we live, and it is a lovely activity to do with children. There will be birds in your local area. Where I live, we see a lot of blackbirds, sparrows, wood pigeons, robins, blue tits and sparrows. I have a feeder in my garden and love watching the birds that come to it. I think it's such a shame that bird spotting has a negative name. In 2025, there was a series called Hamza's Hidden Wild Isles on the BBC, which was filmed around the

UK. In the autumn episode, there is a fantastic interview between Hamza and a young black wildlife trust ranger, Lira Valncia, who is the ranger for Walthamstow Wetlands in London. They talk about their joy of birding, and she describes how people are surprised when they discover she is a wildlife ranger, and how she loves to show it is for everyone. If you haven't seen the series, it is worth watching. The scene in the spring episode of the dawn chorus was magnificent.

I am also tracking the seasons with birds; we have swallows that migrate here. Over the last few years, I have kept a note on my phone of when I see the first swallow of the year. It has been getting earlier, this year it was 14 April, back in 2017 it was 23 April. In the winter, you can see a starling murmuration from November to February. This is when they fly in a large group and appear to dance together in the sky. It's incredible to see. The local area where we can see this is at an RSPB reserve called Ham Wall in Somerset. On the Countryfile website, they have a page describing murmurations, and they have a video of one and a link to places across the UK where you can see this. If you haven't seen a murmuration, take a look at the video.

Did you know?

Migrating swallows cover over 200 miles a day, at speeds of 17–22 mph.

Moment for reflection

Do you know which birds regularly visit your area?

Another way of spotting birds is to take part in the Big Garden Birdwatch. I do this every year with the children I support. You can do it in your own garden or at a park; it takes place every January, and you can find details on the RSPB website.

This year, I discovered a free app called Merlin Bird ID, which is so useful; it identifies birds for you by recording their sound. You press the microphone on the app, and it will record the sounds of the birds you can hear where you are and list what they are. By using this, I discovered we have many chiffchaffs in the meadow that I regularly walk around.

If you would like to attract more birds into your garden, you can easily do this by having a bird feeder. You can also put feeders on balconies and on windows, enabling you to enjoy birds even if you don't have a garden. You can make your own bird feeder. This is a great activity to do with children

Bird feeder instructions

You need

1 large empty plastic drinks bottle
Bird seed
Scissors
String

Instructions

Make a hole at the side of the bottle, around 8 cm.
Make a few small holes in the bottom to act as drainage.
Pour into the bird feeder.
Hang from a tree or window.

Did you know?

The robin is one of the few birds to sing all year round, it's one of the first to start the dawn chorus and one of the last to stop singing at night.

Tree climbing

When I was discussing this chapter with my family, my youngest daughter told me I had to have a section about tree climbing. I don't climb trees as I have a fear of heights, but my daughters and husband are all keen climbers. Below is Summer's explanation for tree climbing:

My favourite outdoor wellbeing activity is tree climbing – you just can't feel low when scampering up a tree. The physical act of climbing a tree concentrates the mind on a puzzle – how do you get up the tree – and the feel of the bark against your hands and knees is very grounding. Also, there's pure joy in stumbling across the perfect tree for climbing and deciding spontaneously to climb it. When up the tree, it is time to relax, watch the dappled sunlight falling through the leaves, admire spiders and other insects crawling around their treetop home, and startle any walkers who happen to glance up and notice you.

If you would like to allow the children you work with to climb trees but have some questions around this, the Forest School Association have a useful page with ideas.

Did you know?

Tree climbing can help lower stress and anxiety, and help improve problem-solving skills.

Finding joy in nature

I think there is so much joy to be found while being in nature, from seeing wild animals and birds, finding free food, experiencing the spring sun warming our faces and picking blackberries. I would argue one of the easiest ways to find some joy is by being in nature.

Conclusion

Hopefully, this chapter has offered a few ideas of ways to engage in nature, whether for yourself or ways you can do more of this at work. I know I am totally biased, as I love being out in nature. If nature is not normally your thing, then I hope that perhaps there could be an idea of something that you might try.

Ideas on how to incorporate this into early years practice and at home

- Have an area where you can grow plants with children, or if you don't have the space for this, use some pots. Bulbs are great for planting in the autumn (be aware that daffodil bulbs are poisonous to eat, so be mindful if you have children who put things in their mouths). You could plant potatoes in pots or beans. Involve the children in planting and looking after the plants.
- Set up a bird spotting area, have some bird feeders and print off some spotting sheets.
- Make a bug house. BBC Bitesize has a link on how to do this.
- Go for a walk in your local area, find out what grows locally, and you could keep a list throughout the year of the different plants and animals you find. You could use the Merlin app to identify any bird song.
- Have some plants inside your setting or home. You could see if anyone in your community has some plants they could share with you, and involve the children in looking after the plants.
- If there are blackberries in your local area, go on a walk to pick them and then make an apple and blackberry crumble with the children.

If you have

If you have 2 minutes, stand outside and see if you can see any wildlife/flowers/trees, or just look at the sky and do some cloud spotting. Breathe deeply.

If you had 10 minutes, you could try and go for a short walk, if you get the chance, hug a tree, or if that feels too weird, just touch it and notice the texture of the bark. If you want an extra boost, try barefoot walking.

If you had 20 minutes, you could try and plant some seeds or a bulb. You don't need a garden, you can grow something on your windowsill, or buy a herb plant and split it so you have more than one to grow on your windowsill and share the other with a friend.

If you had 40 minutes, you could try and go for a longer walk, maybe somewhere new, and use the Merlin app to discover what birds are in the area you're walking.

Links to walks

South west

Mells circular walk: https://www.greatbritishlife.co.uk/magazines/somerset/24109214.somerset-health-walk-mells-three-mile-circular-route/
North Somerset coastal path: https://www.nationaltrust.org.uk/visit/somerset/sand-point/things-to-see-and-do-at-sand-point-and-middle-hope
Bath – Little Solsbury hill: https://www.bathscape.co.uk/activity/little-solsbury-hill-circular/
Somerset levels: https://www.rspb.org.uk/days-out/reserves/ham-wall
Bristol – Badocks Wood: https://www.bristol.gov.uk/residents/museums-parks-sports-and-culture/parks-and-open-spaces/nature-reserves/badocks-wood
Gloucester: https://theoutdoorguide.co.uk/walking-routes/walks-by-region/south-west-england/walks-in-gloucestershire/gloucester-and-sharpness-canal/
Wiltshire – Shearwater Lake: https://hiiker.app/trails/england/wiltshire/shearwater-lake-walk
Devon: https://dartmoorwalking.org/p/buckland-beacon-ten-commandments-stone/
Dorset: https://www.dorsetwalks.co.uk/highcliffe-to-mudeford-quay-walk/
South Cornwall: https://www.cornwalls.co.uk/walking/the-tinners-way.htm
North Cornwall: https://www.southwestcoastpath.org.uk/walksdb/674/

South east

London – Richmond Park: https://www.royalparks.org.uk/visit/parks/richmond-park

London Capital Ring Walk: https://tfl.gov.uk/modes/walking/capital-ring
New Forest: https://newforestwalks.co.uk/walks/coppice-of-linwood.html/
Essex: https://www.komoot.com/smarttour/e996725159/dedham-constable-country-loops-of-flatford-dedham-vale
Oxford: https://www.parks.ox.ac.uk/walks

East of England

Cambridge – Wandlebury Country Park: https://cambridgeppf.org/wandlebury-country-park/
Suffolk – Woodbridge circular walk: https://www.nationaltrust.org.uk/visit/suffolk/kyson-hill/kyson-hills-marshes-mudflats-and-woodbridge-walk
Herefordshire: https://www.cpreherts.org.uk/discover/the-harcamlow-way/

West Midlands

Worcestershire – Malvern Hills: https://www.visitthemalverns.org/things-to-do/walking/walk-finder/?wpv-walk-location=walks-on-the-malverns
Shropshire: https://www.forestryengland.uk/wyre-forest/walking-trails-wyre
Birmingham: https://canalrivertrust.org.uk/things-to-do/walking/canal-and-river-walks-near-me/birmingham-canal-walk-livery-street-to-the-mailbox

East Midlands

Leicestershire: https://www.nationalforest.org/explore/woodlands/the-outwoods
Derbyshire: https://theoutdoorguide.co.uk/walking-routes/walks-by-region/east-midlands/derbyshire/nine-ladies-stone-circle-peak-district/
Lincolnshire: https://www.lincsfenlands.org.uk/lincolnshire-fens/

Yorkshire and Humber region

Sheffield: https://www.welcometosheffield.co.uk/content/attractions/five-weirs-walk/?
West Yorkshire: Ilkley Moor https://www.ilkleymoor.org/heritage-walks/
Huddersfield: https://www.walkingenglishman.com/westyorkshire14.html
York: Askham Bog https://www.ywt.org.uk/nature-reserves/askham-bog-nature-reserve

North west

Cheshire – Whitegate Way: https://visitcheshire.com/trails/the-whitegate-way
Cumbria – Rannerdale Knotts: https://www.thelakedistrict.org/things-to-do/walks/rannerdale-knotts/
Lancashire – Pendle Hill walk: https://www.thewalkingnortherners.co.uk/pendle-hill-walk-from-barley/
North Cumbria: https://www.walkingbritain.co.uk/walk-3552-description

North east

Lindisfarne: https://visitlindisfarne.com/listings/attractions-activities/north-shore-walk/
Hadrian's Wall walk: https://www.nationaltrust.org.uk/visit/north-east/hadrians-wall-and-housesteads-fort/housesteads-to-steel-rigg-circular-walk
Kielder Forest walks: https://www.forestryengland.uk/kielder-forest/walking-trails-kielder-forest

Wales

Brecon Beacons: https://www.breconbeacons.org/things-to-do/walking
Tor y Foel mountain: https://www.gps-routes.co.uk/routes/home.nsf/RoutesLinksWalks/tor-y-foel-walking-route
Gower coast: https://ohwhataknight.co.uk/blog/three-cliffs-bay-walk
Pembrokeshire: https://www.nationaltrust.org.uk/visit/wales/st-davids-peninsula/st-davids-head-coastal-walk

Scotland

Glasgow: https://www.citycentremuraltrail.co.uk/
Isle of Lewis: https://www.visitouterhebrides.co.uk/routes/around-the-butt-of-lewis-p521911
Isle of Harris: https://www.visitouterhebrides.co.uk/routes/northton-machair-and-temple-p521381
Orkney – Yesnaby-Stromness: https://www.northlinkferries.co.uk/orkney-blog/yesnaby-to-skaill/

Edinburgh: https://www.travelswithakilt.com/arthurs-seat-walk-map/
Ochils: https://fifewalking.com/find-a-walk/ochils/
Iona: https://www.walkhighlands.co.uk/mull/iona-north.shtml

References

120 minutes in nature: https://www.nature.com/articles/s41598-019-44097-3#Abs1

BBC Bitesize: https://www.bbc.co.uk/bitesize/articles/z3r346f

BBC Countryfile magazine: https://www.countryfile.com/go-outdoors/walks/walking-groups-for-people-with-disabilities

BBC Country file elderflowers: https://www.countryfile.com/how-to/elderflower-guide-where-to-find-it-how-to-identify-and-recipe-ideas

BBC Good Food: https://www.bbcgoodfood.com/glossary/elderberries-glossary

Big garden bird watch: https://www.rspb.org.uk/whats-happening/big-garden-birdwatch

Black girls hike: https://www.bghuk.com/

Canal River Trust: https://canalrivertrust.org.uk/things-to-do/canal-and-river-wildlife/a-spotters-guide-to-waterway-wildlife/identifying-wildlife/rose-hips

Early Morning Walk – *Just one thing*: https://www.bbc.co.uk/sounds/play/m000v3fz

Environment Agency: https://environmentagency.blog.gov.uk/2021/08/04/blue-space-the-final-frontier/

Forest school association: https://forestschoolassociation.org/climbing-trees-and-rocks/

Gardeners' World Hyacinth: https://www.gardenersworld.com/how-to/how-to-grow-hyacinths/#indoors

Gardeners' World: https://www.gardenersworld.com/

Green social prescribing: https://www.england.nhs.uk/personalisedcare/social-prescribing/green-social-prescribing/

Hamza's Hidden Wild Isles: https://www.bbc.co.uk/iplayer/episodes/p0l07b2y/hamzas-hidden-wild-isles

Intelligent Health: https://- www.intelligenthealth.co.uk/wp-content/uploads/2025/03/Nature-health-wellbeing.-The-benefits-and-practice-of-Green-Social-Prescribing.pdf

Landgirls: https://landgirlsgowalking.substack.com/
Lasagne bulb planting: https://growingfamily.co.uk/garden-tips/plant-bulb-lasagne/
Living Streets: https://www.livingstreets.org.uk/get-involved/local-groups
Mabey, R. (2012). *Food for free*. Collins. London
National Academy for Social Prescribing: https://socialprescribingacademy.org.uk/read-the-evidence/nature/
RHS health and wellbeing: https://www.rhs.org.uk/advice/health-and-wellbeing
RHS house plants: https://www.rhs.org.uk/plants/types/houseplants/for-human-health
RHS wellbeing and gardening: https://www.rhs.org.uk/advice/health-and-wellbeing/articles/why-gardening-makes-us-feel-better
Starling murmuration: https://www.countryfile.com/wildlife/birds/what-is-a-murmuration-and-where-are-the-best-places-in-britain-to-see-one
Three-cornered leek: https://www.wildwalks-southwest.co.uk/all-about-three-cornered-leek/
Walking Men: https://thewalkingmen.com/
Wild garlic: https://www.bbcgoodfood.com/howto/guide/how-to-use-wild-garlic
Woodland Trust – foraging tips: https://www.woodlandtrust.org.uk/visiting-woods/things-to-do/foraging/
Woodland Trust – honeysuckle: – https://www.woodlandtrust.org.uk/blog/2021/06/foraging-in-june/
Woodland Trust – crab apples: https://www.woodlandtrust.org.uk/trees-woods-and-wildlife/british-trees/a-z-of-british-trees/crab-apple/

3 Exercise

We all know that exercise is important; we are all encouraged to find some form of exercise to engage in. This chapter is going to briefly look at why exercise is important for our wellbeing and the research on this. Then I am going to explore different examples of exercise. For most of this chapter, I am drawing on other people's stories and experiences of engaging in exercise.

The NHS guidance for adults between the ages of 19 and 64 is that we should aim to:

Do strengthening activities that work all the muscle groups at least twice a week.
Do 150 minutes of moderate intensity a week or 75 minutes of vigorous intensity a week.

There are a wide variety of ways we can engage in moderate intensity or vigorous exercise, from running, swimming, dancing, walking up stairs, cycling, gymnastics, martial arts, team sports such as football, rugby, hockey, to list a few.

We know that exercise is important for our physical wellbeing, but it's also great for our mental health. The Mind website suggests that physical activity can:

Improve sleep
Help with stress
Help manage feelings of depression and anxiety
Improve mood
Help with memory and brain function

DOI: 10.4324/9781003717591-4

For me, the key with exercise is finding your thing, something that you enjoy; or to start with, that you're willing to give a go in the hope that you will find some joy! It took me a long time to find my thing, and to be honest, I didn't try very hard for a long time! I hated sport at school, I'm dyspraxic and loathe anything to do with catching. I quite liked running, but as an adult, I didn't engage with this as my dad and sister were good marathon runners, and I didn't want to do the same as them (I'm sure that says a lot about me). I'm scared of bikes after falling off several times, and being near cars on a bike terrifies me. I eventually decided to start swimming in my late 30s, and after six months, I fell in love with it.

For the rest of this chapter, I am going to be exploring various sports, with a variety of voices talking about their sport and how it makes them feel.

Moment for reflection

Before we continue, just take a moment to think about how you feel about exercise. It might be something that immediately fills you with a sense of enjoyment, or you might be someone who feels a sense of dread at the word. Our feelings about exercise are sometimes impacted by negative memories of sport at school.

Swimming

I am starting this section with my experience of swimming. Anyone who has read my books before and knows me will know I love swimming. I swim at my local pool five mornings a week. I am in the pool with five other women at 6.20 am every Monday–Friday. I swim for around 30 minutes, I am not particularly fast, and neither do I have the best swimming style, my breast stroke is still wonky! But for me, it's not about speed, it's about the time to let go. On some swims I work hard and push my body, as I know my body is full of stress and needs to release it; on other swims I go gently as I know my body is tired and I just need the water to hold me. Alongside the love of being in the water, the other big plus is the community and friendship with the five other women. I didn't start swimming to make friends, but that has been an unexpected bonus to the swims. In the changing rooms before and after, there is often much laughter, sometimes tears and a sense of being looked out for within our small group. There is also a refreshing honesty around bodies, which at first I found surprising, and I have learnt to love and be hugely grateful for. I know for some, the idea of getting changed in a public changing room can feel awful, and it will fill many with a sense of dread. I was a little cautious at first, but soon realised nobody cares, nobody is looking at you, and it's far easier and quicker to strip off and be done with it!

One of the things I love about swimming is that it is an exercise that uses most of the muscle groups. It is seen as being a great all-around activity that is good for cardiovascular, muscle strength and building endurance without putting too much strain on the body.

I have been told by some that swimming is a white, middle-class activity, and I absolutely hear that to go swimming is not free; there is a cost to buying costumes and goggles, and to pay for the pool. It's also becoming harder to access a pool in some areas, as sadly, since COVID, many public swimming pools have been closing down. In 2019, Swim England released statistics saying 1 in 3 adults in the UK could not swim 25 metres (1 length of a pool). Swimming has been part of the primary curriculum since 1994, with an expectation that all 11-year-olds should leave primary school being able to:

- Perform safe self-rescue in different water-based situations.
- Swim competently, confidently and proficiently over a distance of at least 25 metres.
- Use a range of strokes effectively, for example, front crawl, backstroke and breaststroke.

However, since 2012, Swim England has been monitoring the provision being offered and has found that, consistently, only half the pupils meet these standards. Swim England has resources on their website to offer guidance to schools regarding this. Even if you don't want to swim regularly, knowing how to swim is such an important life skill.

I really believe swimming should be accessible for all, and as part of the research for this book, I have been looking for examples of this. In the summer of 2025, I went on a study visit to a fantastic exhibition at the Design

Museum in London called Splash, which celebrated a love of water. One of the films in the show was of a group called The Subversive Sirens, who have reclaimed synchronised swimming in the name of Black liberation, body acceptance and queer visibility. In the references, I have linked to a film about them on YouTube; they are such a joyful group of women, and I recommend you watch the 5-minute film.

It is often said that Black people don't swim. In the Splash exhibition, they had some slides on this issue. One statistic was that Black children drown at a rate that's 5.5 times greater than other children. The source for this in the exhibition was from the Centers for Disease Control and Prevention (CDC), it's an American statistic. There is a group in the UK (I also discovered them at the Splash exhibition) called Swim Dem Crew. They are based in London, and they describe themselves as a swimming collective that has created sessions for people to learn to swim. They were set up by three friends, Nathaniel, Peigh and Emily. They were particularly aware that there were barriers for Black people to swim; they wanted to create a space for all people from all abilities and backgrounds, and to help improve accessibility and to help move the mainstream attention from the narrative that swimming is mainly for white people. They also have a short film about their collective called Beyond the Blue. It's a wonderful and encouraging short film to watch; the link for this is also in the references. There is an excellent interview with them on the Thiiird magazine website about why they think in the UK there is this idea that Black people don't swim. The interview recognises that there are some extra aggravations for Black people swimming (hair care and skin care), but it also concedes that this is a very Western view and presumption that Black people don't swim, and how in other countries swimming is often viewed differently. To be fair, this might also be about warmth. I totally understand how swimming in the sea in Trinidad, where it is warm and beautiful, must be more appealing than swimming in a cold pool in the UK!

There are a growing number of swim groups appearing across the UK. I recently heard of one in Bristol called Open Minds Active, which is a social enterprise project aiming to strengthen mental health and wellbeing within communities by reducing health inequalities and widening access to nature and blue spaces. They particularly aim to work with people who haven't swum or don't have easy access to swimming. They run swimming lessons for women from diverse ethnic backgrounds, and they have local GPs who social refer patients to their wild swimming wellbeing groups. It is such an inspiring organisation.

Did you know?

The earliest evidence of swimming comes from Egypt. There is a 10,0000-year-old rock that has carvings of swimmers, it's called the cave of swimmers in the Sahara Desert. It's worth looking at the photo of them.

Outdoor swimming

To conclude this section on swimming (I could write a whole chapter on just swimming), I want to write about outdoor swimming. This has become a huge part of my life. I love outdoor swimming; there is something about the combination of being outside and in the water that's perfect for me. Swimming outside on a sunny day when the sun is reflecting on the water, you can see trees around you and hear birds, it's so joyful. But since peri-menopause hit, I have also learnt to crave the cold water. I now swim all year outdoors, at least once a week and sometimes more. I swim in the sea, rivers, lakes, lidos, sea pools and ponds. I have also been known to swim in shallow brooks if I am feeling desperate! I swim in what is described as skins, which means a costume rather than a wetsuit, but I also use swim shoes in the summer, as I hate the feel of mud/stones under my feet and in the winter I swim with wetsuit 5 mm boots and wetsuit 5 mm gloves. This gives some protection from the cold. I have found outdoor swimming to be the best stress relief, and I think it has helped with some of my menopause symptoms. There is something about getting into the water, and my brain switches off from whatever is filling it. When the water is cold, your brain is taken up initially with deep breathing and being aware of how cold it feels on the body, and then you notice how beautiful your surroundings are. Life and work can feel incredibly challenging. I often find that my job in schools and nurseries leaves me with a head full of voices and stories and problems to solve, so being outside in water helps me to find some quiet and peace. I have learnt over the years that prioritising opportunities to be in cold water is the most loving thing I can do for myself.

Of course, swimming outdoors comes with some risks. I am really careful, and I have learnt to know my body and recognise what my body is telling me, for example not getting too cold, but I have also learnt to read the environment. Sadly, one big risk in the UK is water quality. The organisation Surfers Against Sewage has an excellent app called Safer Seas and River Service, and it will tell you of any warnings in the area you are planning to swim. In the winter, I mainly swim in a private pond near where I live, and also the marine lake at Clevedon, which is a large sea pool free to all. Both of these are safer for swimming as they are not affected by tides/fast-running water.

If outdoor swimming is something you would like to try, below are a few tips and guidelines.

- Make sure you can swim at a basic level! This sounds obvious, but you would be surprised how many people enter water without a basic level of swimming.
- Check the water! If it is a river, look for how fast it is moving. Know the tides if it is the sea, and look for waves, rip currents. Make sure you know how to get in and get out.
- Swim with others.
- Don't jump in; allow your body to get used to it.
- Be visible in the water, some people wear bright-coloured hats or have a tow float.
- Don't drink alcohol before getting into the water.
- Be aware of the water quality.

There is different advice about how long to stay in the water; the basic rule is not very long when it is cold. Some say a minute per temperature, but I think that can be dangerous advice because 10 minutes at 10 degrees if you're just starting can be too long, and you might get hypothermia. Sometimes I am just in for a few minutes. I swam yesterday, and it was 9 degrees in the water and 4 degrees outside. I only swam for around 5 minutes; I knew that was enough. You need to remember that your core temperature drops after you get out of the water. Outdoor Swimmer has an excellent article about swimming temperatures and guidance. I like their temperature gauge.

0–5 degrees	Technical term	Bloody freezing
5–10 degrees	Technical term	Effing cold
10–15 degrees	Technical term	Nippy, not as "warm as we like it"
15–20 degrees	Technical term	Balmy
25–30 degrees	Technical term	Stifling
30 degrees plus	Technical term	Hot

If you are swimming outdoors in the winter, make sure you:

Have a warm drink immediately after the swim
Have a warm hat and gloves to put on
Put on lots of layers
Get dressed quickly

For more information on safe swimming outdoors, do have a look at the outdoor swimmer website, linked in the references.

I am not the only early years educator who likes swimming outdoors

Sarah on outdoor swimming

The breath-stealing cold of rivers and lakes definitely keeps me mentally well. Outdoor swimming restores balance for me and gives me a sense of perspective.

Kerry on lido swimming

For my own mental wellness, I swim at my local lido. As an autistic person, I find being in water to be one of my sensory glimmers. It is the only environment where my nervous system feels soothed, especially with it being outdoors and there being lots of space.

Sauna and cold water dips

Over the last few years, there has been an increase in mobile saunas popping up, often by lakes, rivers and coastal areas. The Scandinavians have a long history of sauna and cold dipping. Many people who engage in this regularly feel it boosts their mental wellbeing, and others believe it can help some health conditions, such as blood pressure. There is very limited scientific research on this area, but it is being increasingly looked at. For further information on this, the BBC had an article on their website, linked in the references. Having a daughter who lives in Oslo, I have been very fortunate to experience the sauna culture there, and it is so popular. Oslo has many floating saunas on the fjord. There is something incredibly relaxing about being in a sauna, overlooking a fjord and then dipping in the water when the air temperature is –7, and the water is around –1. If you like the idea of a sauna but you're a bit worried about the cold water dip, you don't have to do that bit; you can stand outside to cool down, or have a shower. Most of the mobile saunas in the UK have websites, and on their websites, they often have guidance notes. If you have a health condition or are pregnant, you are advised to speak to a GP first before you try this.

To finish off this section, I am recommending some outdoor spaces to swim, the ones I am suggesting are lidos and sea pools that I have swum in. These are excellent places to swim; some lidos are open all year round and have lifeguards, and you still get the joy of being outside and in water without the worry of tides or currents. Sea pools often don't have lifeguards, so of course, you need to be safe aware, but they are free, and they don't have currents or tides to worry about. There is an increasing number of lidos and sea pools reopening as the interest in outdoor swimming is increasing. These are also excellent and safer for doing outdoor swimming with children.

Clevedon Marine Lake (sea pool) near Bristol
Greenbank pool (lido) in Somerset
Shepton Mallet (lido) in Somerset
Bude sea pool in North Devon
Jubilee Pool (lido) in Penzance, Cornwall
Chapel sea pool in St Just, Cornwall
Tinside lido in Plymouth
Heathersage swimming pool (lido) in Derbyshire
Brockwell lido in London
Hampstead Heath bathing ponds in London
Serpentine in London
Hinksey outdoor pool in Oxford
Saltdean lido in Brighton
Nantwich outdoor brine pool in Cheshire

Shap swimming pool (lido) in Cumbria

There is a useful website listing all the lidos and sea pools in the UK, linked in the references.

Moment for reflection

When was the last time you swam? Is it something that brings you joy or fills you with horror? If you have children, do you take them swimming?

Running

Running is absolutely not my thing! I have tried it and disliked it. For this section, I have approached two people I know well who love running.

Some of my family are runners: my dad was in the police, and he took up running at 30 and ran many marathons, Ironman competitions, and numerous relay events across the world. Running was a way to help him switch off and destress. My sister is also a runner; she worked for the police and now works in social services in Orkney, and running is a massive stress relief for her. Below are her thoughts about running.

Karen's thoughts on running

I'm quite lucky, my love of running incorporates nature and culture often all in one hit!

In January, I set myself the goal of running (outdoors only!) every day for the month of January, regardless of the weather. In Orkney, this is more difficult than it sounds.

Despite extreme weather conditions, including gales, ice, snow and torrential rain, my commitment to the process and endurance of the elements reignited my love of running. (This hasn't really faded over the last 30-odd years, but it gave it a new light and enthusiasm.)

I try to run first thing in the morning, when I take Alfie to swim training at 6 am. I love the sense of achievement that running so early gives me.

Living on such a small Island, we are never far from the sea, so for me, every run takes in a beach or cliff top and finishes at a bay where I take a quick dip in the sea. I now cherish the sea dip as much as my runs. The water heals my ageing limbs and aches, and it totally grounds me for the day ahead.

One of my shorter runs is around the Ring of Brodgar and down to the loch side. I get to run among some amazing history and occasionally spot otters along the way. This is a total cultural and historical immersion within my exercise!

A friend of mine, Jenny Baker, is a runner, and she has written a book: *Run for your life: How one woman ran circles around breast cancer* (2017). The book is about running while going through cancer treatment. She has written her thoughts on how running supports her wellbeing.

Running and wellbeing: Jenny

Work has been stressful lately, with lots to do, difficult decisions to make, and elusive funding to find. My mind is a churn of thoughts that are hard to quiet. So I put on my trainers and head out of the door. The rhythm of my feet hitting the streets and the fresh air filling my lungs begins to soothe me almost immediately. I settle into a steady pace, nothing fast or fancy, and head towards the river. Gradually, the run works its magic, untangling my thoughts, drawing them back from anxiety about the future into the here and now. This is what is real: legs, arms and breath working together. My mind starts to relax, to become curious, to gain a different perspective. And I arrive back home ready to face the day.

Running has been a good friend to me for nearly 30 years, improving my mental and physical health, helping me cope with the ups and downs of life. Getting started can feel daunting if you've never done it before, but my tip is to start slowly and to combine running and walking. Try a slow jog for two minutes, followed by walking for a minute and repeat that a few times. A few days later, run for three minutes and walk for one with one more repetition, gradually increasing the amount of time you're out on your feet, and the proportion of it that you're running. Celebrate what you have achieved. You can find apps that will guide you, or head to your local parkrun one Saturday morning, where people of all abilities will be turning up to experience the joy of running. Some running clubs organise beginner's sessions where friendly volunteers run and walk with you. You don't have to be a "real" runner to join; you might find you are by the end.

Women are always vigilant about safety when out and about. Running is no exception, and finding a buddy to run with can help while you build your confidence. Choose well-lit streets and avoid secluded places; you know the score. Ignore ignorant catcalls or any comments about your body; you're strong and getting stronger. And while we need to be aware, don't let fear keep you inside or stop you from benefiting from the gift of running.

How to get started

If running is something you like the idea of trying, but you're not sure where to start, Couch to 5K might be the place for you. It is a free app you can download, which guides you through a running plan. It was created between the BBC Sport and the Department of Health and Social Care. It is a nine-week structured program aimed at people who have never run before. The program has you running three times a week, it has rest days in between and a new schedule for each week. A trainer guides you through your head-phones at the start of the program. You start with 1-minute runs and then a 1 minute and 30 second walk. The aim is to gradually increase your stamina and confidence. I know several people who have used this app to get started and found it really useful.

Park runs

Park runs are free community events which take place across the UK (and in many other countries too). They are 5 k in distance, you can run, walk or jog. They take place every Saturday throughout the year, and they have junior parkrun events on Sundays for children aged 4–14; these are 2 k. As I am writing this, according to their website, there are 1,381 parkrun events in the UK. parkrun is a charity, it is volunteer-led, free for all events. They started in 2004 in Bushy Park in London. Paul Sinton-Hewitt started it with 13 friends joining him. Over the years, parkrun has grown across the world, but the idea is that the event will be the same wherever you go.

The principles are weekly, free, for everyone, forever. I have been along to park runs to observe when friends are running, and I have always been struck by how friendly, encouraging and inclusive they are. There is a mix of runners, from experienced runners who do marathons, to others who are starting out, and some people who walk all of it. It has a feeling of welcome and no shame, which I love, it has almost made me think about running again! I also love the idea that you can turn up at any park run, anywhere in the world, and you know how it will work and that you will be welcome no matter what your running ability is. There was an article in *The Guardian* in 2019 where they interviewed Paul Sinton-Hewitt, and he said: *"One of the things that I'm most proud of is that every year the average finish time at parkrun has slowed. That means we are reaching more people for whom physical activity hasn't been the norm".*

There is a link in the references to park runs and where you can find one close to you.

Moment for reflection

Running is one of those exercises you can do for free. Trainers are useful, but when you start out, you don't need lots of specialist kit. Have you tried running? Do you know if you have a park run near you? You might have friends who go there that you could join.

Did you know?

A marathon is 26.2 miles. This is due to the 1908 Olympics, which took place in London. There was a 26-mile course from Windsor Castle to the stadium, but the royal family wanted the finish line in front of the Royal box, so the extra distance needed to be added on.

Cycling

I know nothing about cycling, but my husband, Iain, is a keen cyclist who has a history of doing short rides, but he has also taken part in much longer rides, including an ultra. He writes about why cycling is so good for his wellbeing.

Cycling was the sport of my youth. I rode with a cycling club, Macclesfield Wheelers, in my late teens and early 20s. I did a bit of racing – time trials, road racing and cyclocross in the winter. What I remember most vividly, though, is the camaraderie of riding with friends and the immense sense of freedom and adventure roaming the Cheshire lanes and Pennine hills. Although I continued to ride a bike, it was the gift of a hand-me-down road bike 15 years ago that was my entry back into more serious cycling. I rode a London to Paris charity bike ride, and I was hooked again. I joined a local cycling group and started exploring my own patch in the Mendip and Cotswold hills around Bath. My racing days were over, but I still loved riding in the bunch and the challenge of hanging on in the sprints and even suffering up the climbs, followed by the thrill of the descent!

I find there is nothing like a long bicycle ride to quieten the mind. There is something about the rhythm of pedalling and the immersion in the landscape that is uniquely wonderful. It offers an escape from the stresses and strains of modern life. The bicycle is a machine made to connect to the body; to become aware of the legs working and the heart and lungs processing oxygen, and the digestive system extracting fuel from cake; to feel the sun and the wind and the rain on your face and feel the force of gravity as you travel up and down hills. It is an antidote to the world of screens and thinking. It is also a wonderful tool for problem solving. Somehow, the space it creates allows the mind the freewheeling opportunity to work the problems of life.

The bicycle gives you the ability, under your own power, to travel considerable distances. What might start with a ride to the shops could develop into a ride from Lands End to John O'Groats.

It is also a good low-impact form of exercise that is great for cardio fitness.

How to start?

You will need a bike. Your local bike shop will be the best source of advice about what you need. They will talk you through what kind of machine will suit the riding you want to do, and will be a good source of advice about the local cycling scene. Bikes can be expensive. Many companies are signed up to the "bike to work" scheme, which discounts the tax on a new bike. There is a good second-hand market for bikes, but do your research first so that you buy a machine that will fit you as well as suit your purposes. Unless you are mechanically minded, ask your local bike shop to give it a service to ensure it is roadworthy. If you haven't exercised in a while, it might be a good idea to ask your GP for advice. You don't have to wear Lycra but a good pair of padded shorts is essential if you want to ride for more than an hour or so.

Most places have quiet lanes and cycle routes, which are a good place to gain confidence in riding again. Look at the National Cycling Network and Sustrans for ideas. In Bath, the Two Tunnels Circuit is an easy walking and cycling route ideal for a family day out. Phone apps like Komoot and Ride with GPS have good tools for route planning. To get started, it can be a good idea to find a local cycling group that organises rides suitable for your ability. For the West, try Better by Bike, which has information about cycling groups across all abilities in the West. Cycling clubs often have rides for all abilities, including beginners, and if you have a competitive streak, will offer pathways into racing. British Cycling is a good source of information for all things cycling.

In the next part of this chapter, I am going to be hearing from a range of people, most of whom work in education, describing their exercise of choice and how it helps them.

Did you know?

There are more cyclists in Copenhagen than drivers; the city is so well set up for cyclists. Traffic jams in the morning are with cyclists, not drivers.

In the next section, we are going to hear a range of voices about favoured exercise and how it find it supports them

Yoga – Kate

I've been going to yoga classes since 2007, and it has been my go-to and consistent exercise throughout that time.

I've had three different teachers, all of whom have had their own district style and approaches. Each one has suited where I was at those points in my life.

The yoga teacher I have now teaches Hatha and Yin yoga and is totally brilliant. She is always kind, sensitive and brings humour to the class. She challenges us but also understands that we will all manage the poses and balances in a way that works for us.

Her lessons often reflect the changes in the seasons or moon cycles. So many times her sessions seem to be just what I need at that time, both for my emotional and mental health as well as my physical wellbeing. Yoga has got me through some pretty tough times in my life, and it's allowed me to move through these experiences and come out the other side.

The hour a week of yoga is so important to me, and if I can't get to class, I really miss it. I miss not just the benefits I get from the yoga practice, but also the people who go to the class. It is like our own mini community, and it feels very special.

Hockey – Ruth

I work at the University of Suffolk, where I am Professor in Diagnostic Radiography and Head of Allied Health Professions. It is quite a busy and at times stressful job. I find that sport is a really good coping mechanism, and as well as running every morning, I also play hockey. Not only does this help with fitness and agility, but it also helps to play a team sport with others. Our hockey team is made up of women from different backgrounds, jobs and interests, but we all come together as a team to play hockey. It is a social and fun sport, and together we learn to play as a team and support one another. I find it a great way to let off steam, and I also know that my teammates have my back both on and off the field. After the game, we have tea together and vote for the player of the match. We train for an hour once a week and then play every Saturday. You can take out your frustrations on the ball by hitting it hard as well!

Karate – Clare

I was always that kid at school who got picked last for team games. It was fair enough, I have no hand-eye coordination to speak of, and I didn't much care about winning! So I formed the opinion very early that I was "bad at sports", and apart from occasional yoga classes, managed to avoid any sport or exercise for most of my adult life. Then I read a book about a female martial artist. The way she wrote about karate made me really want to try it. It seemed a bit ridiculous as an idea, but it didn't go away, so I did a Google search. I found a club five minutes' walk from my house. "Beginners welcome, First session free". I messaged them, half-expecting to be told that at 55 I was too old to be a beginner – but they encouraged me to go along, and I'm so glad I did. Turns out, I love karate. I feel amazing after my training sessions, in a way I have never experienced before. It has been the single best thing I've ever done for my mental health –- the combination of concentration and physical hard work is tiring but also gives me energy. My only regret is that I didn't discover it sooner. Just goes to show that it is always worth trying something new.

Team sports – Katie

Team sports run through my veins from an early age. My dad was always involved in football and cricket, as was my grandad. I was always in and among it and have loved going to watch Derby County with my dad throughout my life. But being part of an actual team has always been a passion of mine, and as I reflect, I can't remember a time when I wasn't. School netball and rounders teams offered the first experience of what it was all about. As an adult, I continued playing netball for various teams, and then at 31, I had my daughter Zoe. Fast forward to when she was 8, and I took her to Belper Amateurs Cricket Club for training. While I was watching at the side, some of the mums were having a training session. Women's softball had been introduced to get women interested in playing cricket. The following week I made sure I had my trainers and joined in. The rest is history. What an amazing eight years. Richard Cope, our coach/manager, who is an excellent cricketer, patiently turned us into a cricket team. Festivals, softball league, East Midlands Championships and a transition to hardball, which I never imagined I would play. All this with an amazing group of players who I am proud to call friends. When my daughter turned 12, she joined our team, and we have trained together, batted together and created so many amazing memories. The highlight of it all was in September 2024 when we played in the East Midlands Women's Softball Championship, after winning the league. We won, but that is by the by. We played on hallowed turf with all our family and friends watching on proudly. It's great to win, but how much fun those victories are when you are with friends. In my role as a teacher, I love team sports and encourage as many children as possible to attend an event. These experiences cannot be replicated in school, but they have a positive impact in the classroom. Team sports are brilliant, I cannot advocate for them enough.

Dance – Sam

Sam works in a school and is also a dance teacher for a dance group in Bath
Being part of a dance group, whether it is classical, street or hip hop, is about so much more than simply learning routines.

For young people to learn something new, using their whole body, it's a very vulnerable position to be in. Particularly if the young people easily feel any sense of shame, embarrassment or low confidence about their bodies. So that automatically means a level of trust has to be given to whoever is teaching them and their peers around them.

Once that is overcome and a young person begins to learn a new skill, they gain a sense of achievement in themselves and also as part of a group. This automatically creates a sense of belonging. Friendships through any physical activity grow on a deeper level, experiencing the serotonin high from exercise and sense of achievement create a certain bond, as does struggling through difficult parts of routines and choreography together.

This all goes hand in hand with the physical benefits of dance, muscle memory, muscle strengthening and improved cardio. In my experience, young people leave dance lessons feeling physically tired but uplifted, motivated and satisfied with what they have achieved or overcome.

Climbing – Summer

For me, rock-climbing is great for my wellbeing; however, if you're afraid of heights, then I don't recommend it. Rock-climbing, roped or bouldering, is fairly all-consuming – you have to be in the moment, with all concentration on the wall and your body in relation to it. Climbing throughout my A-Levels was one of the key things I put in place for my wellbeing – it forced my brain to take a rest and flooded my body with endorphins. The satisfaction of completing a tricky move that I'd been practising for weeks and the adrenaline that came from falling off the wall only to be caught by my partner is like no other – and all the better for sharing with friends. That's the other great thing about climbing – it's a social sport! Even bouldering, which doesn't need a partner, is all about sharing a problem and route with those around you – sharing the joy of a tricky route and the satisfaction of completing a climb with the strangers around you.

Fitness classes

If you're in a place where you would like to improve your fitness but don't want to engage in any of the ideas above, doing a fitness class might be the best option for you. There will be fitness classes in your local area and at local gyms. However, if the idea of joining a class or the gym may feel too intimidating, in the way that there is a free Couch to 5k program, there is also a free Couch to Fitness nine-week fitness plan, which you can do from your home. The idea is a free exercise plan to get back into or start exercising. Three fitness instructors take you through 30-minute videos, three times a week.

Moment for reflection

Is there anything in this list of activities that made you think I would like to try that? Or is there a form of exercise you have done in the past you would like to try again?

Activities that brought people joy

From the people I spoke to, a few of them mentioned exercise activities that brought them joy.

Emily – *Definitely aerial hoop and sling.*

Jamel – *Going on walks or riding my bike also helps to lower my stress and these things also bring me joy.*

Alistair – *I really enjoy running and walking. I was a reluctant runner (and when I say "run" it is more of a jaunty jog!), but once I got into it, I found I really liked it. Not only for the challenge of getting a bit further, but also for the thinking time. I had really underestimated the positive impact of just being outside in the fresh air. My favourite time to be out is early in the morning, when everyone else is still asleep.*

Conclusion

There is a range of exercise examples here from different people. Hopefully something in the list caught your attention or reminded you of something you have enjoyed in the past. I do think the key with exercise is to find your thing, or at least what you can tolerate to start with, in the hope you will grow to love it. What I loved about Clare's story is that it's not too late to start something new. I have only written about a few different exercise activities, there are so many ones that can be tried.

Ideas on how to incorporate this into early years practice and at home

- Do some dance together: CBBC and CBeebies have some dance examples you can follow, or make up your own.
- Set up an obstacle course with the children. You can also do this at home or in a garden.
- Use Joe Wicks Activate, it's a CBBC program to introduce short exercise practices aimed at children.
- Go for a short run/walk together, you might have a local field you could run around in.
- Get out and use bikes and scooters in the nursery and at home. As a family, there might be a local cycle path you can find.
- As a family, go to the local swimming pool.

If you have

If you have 2 minutes, do some shoulder rolls. These are great for releasing tension in your neck. Try rolling five times on one shoulder and then do the other. Then repeat this.

If you had 10 minutes, you could put on some music and dance. You can do this in the privacy of your own home, don't worry about your dance moves it's about the freedom of moving and dancing, and hopefully finding some joy.

If you had 20 minutes, you could try a jog in your local area, or if jogging for 20 minutes feels too hard, try a combination of walking and jogging.

If you had 40 minutes, you could try a fitness class either online or go to a class in person or go for a swim at your local pool.

References

All the lidos: https://allthelidos.co.uk/all-the-outdoor-swimming-pools-and-lidos-in-the-uk-the-complete-and-updated-list/

Activate with Joe Wicks: https://www.bbc.co.uk/iplayer/episode/m002j876/activate-with-joe-wicks-series-1-astroburp

BBC Do saunas boost your health? https://www.bbc.co.uk/news/articles/c5yj3g0p26ro

Better by bike: https://betterbybike.info/

Bike to work scheme: https://www.bike2workscheme.co.uk/

British Cycling: https://www.britishcycling.org.uk/

Cave of Swimmers: https://egyptunitedtours.com/cave-of-swimmers/

CBBC dance: https://www.bbc.co.uk/cbbc/curations/the-next-step-dances

CBeebies dance: https://www.bbc.co.uk/iplayer/group/p04z6yrf

Cycling UK: https://www.cyclinguk.org/article/50-family-friendly-cycle-routes-uk

Beyond the blue: www.swimdemcrew.co.uk/beyond-the-blue

Couch to 5k: https://www.nhs.uk/better-health/get-active/get-running-with-couch-to-5k/

Couch to fitness: https://www.nhs.uk/better-health/get-active/home-workout-videos/

Komoot: https://www.komoot.com/

Mind: https://www.mind.org.uk/information-support/tips-for-everyday-living/physical-activity-exercise-and-mental-health/how-are-physical-activity-and-mental-health-connected/

NHS exercise guidance: https://www.nhs.uk/live-well/exercise/physical-activity-guidelines-for-adults-aged-19-to-64/

Open Minds Active: https://www.openmindsactive.org/

Outdoor swimmer safety: https://outdoorswimmer.com/featured/starting-out-basic-guide-to-outdoor-swimming/
Outdoor swimming temperature guidance: https://outdoorswimmer.com/featured/swimming-in-cold-water-a-guide-to-temperature/
parkrun: https://www.parkrun.com/
Ride with GPS: https://ridewithgps.com/
Safer seas and river service: https://www.sas.org.uk/water-quality/sewage-pollution-alerts/safer-seas-rivers-service/?gad_source=1
Subversive Sirens: www.youtube.com/watch?v=gR4MT7jmuGA
Swim England: https://www.swimming.org/swimengland/one-three-adults-cannot-swim/
Swim England curriculum resources: https://www.swimming.org/schools/swimming-national-curriculum/
Thiiird magazine swim dem crew interview: https://www.thiiirdmagazine.co.uk/stories/swim-dem-crew
The Guardian: https://www.theguardian.com/lifeandstyle/2019/oct/04/parkrun-at-15-bigger-more-global-and-slower-than-ever
Walk, Wheel, Cycle Trust: https://www.walkwheelcycletrust.org.uk/find-a-route-on-the-national-cycle-network/?location=null&distance=null&routetype=null

4 Food

I am aware that as I start this chapter, reading about food can be an emotive subject for some people. My hope with this chapter is to highlight how, for some people, food is a nurturing experience, one they share with others and, for some, the process of cooking is a great stress relief. But I also recognise that it isn't the situation for everyone: for some, reading about food might be triggering, upsetting or stressful. Please be kind to yourself, and if now isn't the right time for you to read this, that is fine, skip it and go to another chapter. In this chapter, I will be sharing some up-to-date information about the food we eat and the impact that has on our minds and bodies, but I will also be sharing people's stories and recipes and looking at how we can eat well on small budgets and in busy lives.

Food and its impact on our minds

We have known for a long time that food can impact our minds. Here are a few key recommendations:

- Eating regularly throughout the day stops your blood sugar level from dropping; if it does drop, it can make you feel tired and grumpy.
- Staying hydrated helps our minds. Mild dehydration can affect our mood, energy level and ability to concentrate.
- Our brain needs healthy fats to work well. Examples of these are found in olive oil, nuts, seeds, avocados, milk, eggs and oily fish. We want to avoid trans fats, which are not good for our hearts and our mood; these are often found in ultra-processed food.

DOI: 10.4324/9781003717591-5

- Grains, fruit and vegetables contain the vitamins and minerals we need for our brain and body health.
- Protein has an amino acid which helps our brain. You can find protein in vegetables and pulses (peas, beans and lentils), nuts and seeds, milk, fish, eggs, cheese, lean meat and soya products.
- There is a link between our gut health and our mental health. Healthy food for our gut includes fermented food, fruit and vegetables and beans.
- Caffeine can impact our mood, and it can cause sleep problems. For some people, it can make them irritable and anxious.

For information around the food we eat and our mental health, the Mental Health Foundation has some useful information on their website. Also, the NHS has the Eatwell Guide on their website, which offers advice around food groups and how to have a healthy, balanced diet.

Thirty plant-based foods a week

Over the last few years, research has developed in the area of food, our gut health and mental health. One of the suggestions is that we need to aim to eat 30 plant-based foods a week. The main reason behind this is improving our gut health. It is believed that if we improve our gut health, then this will also help our mental and physical health. It is about increasing the variety of plant foods we eat, which improves gut health. Dr Tim Spector, who is the co-founder of Zoe, a health science company that leads research around nutrition and gut health, was one of the first groups to start recognising the importance of 30 plant-based foods. When I initially heard this figure, I was concerned it would be very hard to reach and expensive. However, I realised quite quickly that it is achievable and it doesn't have to be costly. Some examples of what this can include are:

- Vegetables
- Fruits
- Pulses, beans, lentils
- Grains (rice, oats, wholegrain flour)
- Nuts and seeds
- Herbs and spices

Also, coffee, tea, herbal teas and dark chocolate all contribute to the 30.

It is also suggested that you want to try and eat as much colour as possible, a red pepper one day and a yellow pepper another day would count as two. I have found that if you cook from scratch and add spices and herbs, this quickly boosts the count. Also, by adding an extra vegetable, for example, if you are making soup from scratch, add in an additional vegetable, or if you are doing a pasta dish, add in some basil or oregano to the sauce, this soon begins to boost the numbers.

For more information on this, there is an article on the Zoe website; a link can be found in the references.

Ultra-processed food

You will have noticed there has been a lot in the press recently about the problems with ultra-processed food. Ultra-processed food is food which has more than one ingredient that you rarely find in your kitchen cupboard, and it also often includes lots of additives, preservatives and emulsifiers, and they generally have a long shelf life. One problem is that there are so many of them on the market now, and often they are cheap.

Some examples of ultra-processed foods are:

Ham and sausages
Mass-produced bread
Breakfast cereal
Instant soup
Crisps
Sweets and chocolate
Biscuits
Ice cream
Fruit-flavoured yoghurts
Carbonated drinks
Diet foods
Plastic-wrapped bread

One of the reasons they are not good for our health is that they contain high levels of saturated fat, sugar and salt; it's also believed they are addictive. New research is also showing that it has a negative impact on our gut health and mental health. The British Heart Foundation has a really useful webpage about this, linked in the references.

Over the last few years, many articles have come out saying we need to eliminate all ultra-processed foods from our diet. And I think ideally that would be great, but in practice, that is incredibly hard to do, and it can be very expensive. I have spent a lot of time thinking and researching this area. The conclusion I have come to for my household is that we try hard to cook from scratch where we can – this includes baking over buying shop-bought cakes and biscuits, and making my own muesli and batch cooking – but we do still eat some ultra-processed food, and we still buy shop-made bread. I think we now eat less ultra-processed food than we did, but we haven't eliminated and if I am honest, I can't see that we will. I do think there is a political issue here that needs addressing. I think the government should be putting more pressure on companies that make these foods, and I have a big concern that it can still be cheaper to buy six bags of crisps than six apples. I also recognise that a lot of these foods are about convenience, and when we are shattered after a hard day's work, we may not have the energy to cook from scratch.

Moment for reflection

Are there ultra-processed foods you eat regularly that you could cut down or cut out? Or maybe you could find a replacement for them?

Recipes

Home-made muesli recipe

Ingredients

400 g oats
100 g brown sugar
Approx. 50 g of dried fruit

Approx. 50 g of nuts
Approx. 25–50 g of seeds
150 ml of water
150 ml of oil (I often use pumpkin seed oil, other times sunflower oil)
Pinch of salt

Instructions

Mix all the ingredients in a bowl.
Put into a baking tray and bake at 200°C/400°F/Gas 6 for 30 minutes.

Home-made flapjack recipe

Ingredients

150 g butter
75 g brown sugar
75 g black treacle
225 g oats
Pinch of salt
50 g of a mix of seeds and dried fruit

Instructions

Melt all the ingredients in a pan
Mix in the oats and stir.
Put into a tin, bake ay at 190 °C/375 F/Gas 5 for 25 minutes.

Fermented food

Another area that is increasingly talked about is fermented food. Along with the growing research into gut health, it is being recognised that fermented food can positively support gut health. Fermented foods include yoghurt (plain, not sweetened ones), kefir, some cheeses (some examples are cheddar, Gouda, Roquefort, camembert, brie), sauerkraut, kimchi and sourdough. The recommendation is to have fermented food little and often, as it positively supports the microbes living in our guts. I need to be honest here, I have tried hard to like fermented food, but I am not a big fan! I like sourdough and cheese and yoghurt, but I haven't yet been convinced by kefir, sauerkraut or kimchi! However, this year I have discovered a recipe for making labneh, which is a Middle Eastern and Mediterranean strained yoghurt dish. You can serve it alongside other dishes as a side dish or dip. For more on fermented food, the BBC have a useful article on their website.

Labneh recipe

Ingredients

1 litre of Greek yoghurt
1 teaspoon of salt

Instructions

Add the salt to the yoghurt and mix.
Pour the yoghurt into a sieve which is lined with a cheesecloth and placed over a bowl.
Strain the yoghurt for around 12–24 hours.
Put the strained mixture into a jar and cover with olive oil. You can add herbs or spices. Keep in the fridge. It is ok for 1–2 weeks.

Did you know?

There is evidence of humans using salt to preserve food from Neolithic times (around 6000 BC), which has been found in Transylvania

Eating well on a small budget

One of the key elements to eating well on a small budget is knowing how to cook from scratch, but also having the time to do this. In 2022, a YouGov survey suggested that only 1 in 3 adults is very confident to cook from scratch without a recipe. It is so much cheaper to eat well and save money if you cook from scratch. As well as the issues about ultra-processed foods in ready meals, as mentioned above, they are also much more expensive. But you have to know how to cook to be able to cook from scratch.

One of the leading voices around cooking on a small budget is Jack Munro. They have several recipe books, and a blog site which has many recipes for free. All their work comes from the experience of being a single mum living on benefits, trying to cook well for themselves and their child. I heard Jack speak at a festival called Greenbelt in 2023; it was a really inspiring talk. The conversation was around their work as an anti-poverty campaigner as well as a food writer. In this conversation, they argue that the rising cost of food inflation and energy prices is making it increasingly hard for many families to be able to eat well, plus the added stresses of many people holding down several jobs, not knowing how to cook. They believe it is a political issue and one that needs to be taken seriously by the government.

While writing this book, I discovered through Emily, one of the contributors who is a childminder in Bath, about an app called Olio. This is an app that enables people to share things that they no longer need, including food. Emily talks about regularly getting surplus vegetables from people in her local area. It was initially set up to combat food waste, but now it also shares other household items. A link to this can be found in the references.

Cooking is a life skill

I think knowing how to cook is such an essential life skill that probably sounds so obvious, but I am aware of many people who don't feel they have those skills. Maybe they didn't learn at school, or were unable to learn from their family. I wonder how many people reach adulthood and are too embarrassed to ask for advice on cooking skills. I do wonder if it is a subject that maybe we are embarrassed to talk about. I am aware that there are often conversations in some workplaces around concerns about the food parents are giving to their children. A question I often ask is: do the parents know how to cook? Do they have the resources they need to be able to cook? I know of some children's centres and schools that have cookery clubs, teaching some basic cooking skills to families and some early years settings that share recipes. I love these ideas.

Moment for reflection

Do you cook with children in your setting or with your children at home? Using simple recipes is a great way to introduce cooking skills.

A good friend of mine, Rachel, works for a children's charity and in her spare time, she teaches cooking to adults in a local rehab hostel based on a farm where they grow many of the ingredients she uses. I have asked her to share a recipe that she has used in her cooking club

Rachel's recipe – Paprika potatoes

This is an economical way to turn potatoes into a delicious meal. I was introduced to this Hungarian dish by a friend when I was a university student, and have been cooking it ever since. As well as a regular dinner dish, it has become a family camping favourite. As you cook it, the potatoes create their own thick sauce. I serve it with sour cream or yoghurt, gherkins, green beans or salad.

Serves 4

Preparation time: 10 minutes
Cooking time: 15–20 minutes

Ingredients

I kg potatoes, peeled and chopped into bitesize pieces
3 onions, sliced and cut into half moons
3 cloves garlic, finely chopped
1 tbsp each of sweet and hot paprika (or 2 tbsp of any paprika)
1.5 tablespoons oil
700 ml water

Salt and pepper to taste
4 soft boiled eggs to accompany the potatoes
Chopped frankfurter sausages to stir in if desired

Instructions

Heat the oil and gently fry the onions and garlic until translucent and tender.
Add paprika and cook for 30 seconds, stirring.
Add potatoes, stir, then add the water (it should just cover the potatoes) and a light seasoning of salt.
Cover and simmer for 10 minutes.
Allow to simmer uncovered for the last 5 minutes, adding in frankfurter sausages if used to warm up.

Kerry shares her thoughts on food

When I first met my husband, he had just made his first sourdough starter. Years later, we have that same starter, and we make sourdough every Friday for weekend magic toast. I also found I feel much better having bread that is home-made, as most shop-bought bread is full of random stuff and makes me feel unwell.

I am autistic and probably known as a beige eater, and I get quite anxious if food changes or does not taste the same. I find mapping out my meals (even though they are mostly the same) on a Sunday helps me to feel anchored during the week and has led me to try new foods. I recently discovered orzo, which is delicious.

How to eat well in a busy working/family life

One of the challenges of working in early years can be the long hours people work and then having the energy to cook at the end of the day. Some people find batch cooking on the weekend a solution to that; others have told me about favourite recipes they turn to, which are easy, quick and comforting, and they can make them without a lot of thought. Soup is a comfort food that several people have mentioned, and can also be batch-cooked. There are a few tips we can take on to help us eat well.

Eat breakfast

Not everyone needs to eat breakfast, but many people find that if they don't, then their energy levels dip as the morning progresses. I know some people who don't have time to eat breakfast at home, but do manage to take breakfast with them and eat it when they get to work. Some suggestions for breakfast are:

Museli
Porridge
Overnight oats
Wholegrain toast with a topping that is not too high in sugar
Yoghurt with fruit and seeds

Plan

Meal planning can help. Preparing a weekly meal plan can save you from the problem of getting home exhausted and not knowing what to cook. It can also help with budgets as you are buying food for the meals you are going to cook, and less likely to waste food.

Batch cooking

I'm not suggesting spending all your weekend cooking, but if you have a freezer and can cook a bit extra, you can freeze these to use as lunch another day or for an evening meal.

Stopping for lunch

I increasingly see staff who work through their lunch break, and if I am honest, I have done this a lot in the past. However, in my current job, I make a conscious effort to stop for lunch and avoid taking it while on my laptop, checking and responding to emails. Even if I only take 20 minutes, it's time to stop, eat slowly, and make sure I am eating. Some suggestions for lunch

Soup
Pasta with pesto and whatever veg is in the fridge
Avocado on toast
Salads
Poached egg on toast
Leftovers from the previous dinner

Staying hydrated

I think this can often be overlooked, particularly when we are busy directly working with children. Keeping a water bottle in the room we are working, and keeping this topped up, is the simplest way to stay hydrated. Staying hydrated supports our cognitive function and supports our mood regulation. The NHS Eatwell Guide suggests adults should aim to drink 6–8 cups or glasses of fluid a day.

Emily shares her thoughts on food and how she tries to make food that is easy and that her childminder children will also eat.

We love a soup using surplus food collected from Olio. One of our favourites is a curried swede, carrot and lentil soup. We always have some in the freezer and often take it in a flask to have for lunch when we're out! I enjoy the flavours and love that I've created something so easily, bulk cooked to save myself prep in the following weeks and so cheaply (only paying for stock and lentils), but it is also nutritious!

Emily's curried soup recipe

Ingredients

800 g swede
2 large carrots
1 onion
3 cloves garlic
200 g red lentils
1 litre vegetable stock
1 tsp chilli flakes
1 tsp coriander powder
1 tsp cumin powder
1 tsp turmeric
1 tbsp sunflower oil

Instructions

Heat the sunflower in a saucepan.
Add onions and garlic and fry for 2–3 minutes.
Tip in the spices and cook for a bit.

Add the swede, carrot and lentils to the pan.
Pour over the stock and bring the soup to the boil.
Reduce the heat, cover, and simmer until the swede, carrot, and lentils are soft.
Blend together.
I vary veg quantities depending on what I have.

Kieran also shared a soup recipe. He has been living in Germany for 30 years, and he manages a kindergarten. He wants food that is easy and quick to make, and he can take it to work for lunch. He says this is a classic German soup recipe.

German potato soup

Ingredients

1 onion
1 leek
1 kg of peeled and chopped potatoes
1 carrot
2 bay leaves
2–4 frankfurters
1 litre of vegetable stock
1 small tub of creme fraiche

Instructions

Sauté one chopped onion and a leek.
Add 1 litre of vegetable stock, a kilo of peeled and chopped potatoes and one chopped carrot and 2 bay leaves.
Cook till the potatoes are very soft.
Remove the bay leaves and purify.
Stir in up to one small carton of creme fraiche.
Chop up 2–4 frankfurters and add to the hot soup.
Season with pepper and chopped parsley.

Quick recipes

Sometimes we need really quick recipes we can turn to that are healthy but super quick to make. My friend Chris shares hers here:

Scrambled tofu

This is one of my favourite midweek suppers. It's really quick to make, packed full of protein and flavour and endlessly versatile – feel free to adjust the veg according to your own personal taste or whatever happens to be lurking in your fridge. I serve this with half an avocado per person, some kimchi or sauerkraut and a simple green salad. It's also great on toast.
Serves 2

Ingredients

1 tbsp coconut or olive oil
1 block extra firm tofu, rinsed and drained
1 red onion, finely sliced
1 red or yellow pepper, sliced
4 spring onions, cut into chunks
1 red chilli (optional), finely diced
1 or 2 cloves garlic, finely chopped
1 large handful parsley or coriander, finely chopped
1 tsp ground turmeric
Tamari to taste
Black pepper to taste

Instructions Heat the oil in a large frying pan, add the onion, pepper, spring onions and chilli and cook until just tender.

Add the chopped garlic and stir through for a minute before crumbling the tofu into the pan (I just use my hands to squish it into little pieces but you can always mash it with a fork in a bowl before adding it to the pan if you prefer).

Add the remaining ingredients to the pan, stir well and adjust the seasoning to taste. Serve and enjoy.

Black bean salad

This simple salad makes a great speedy supper served with a baked sweet potato and a big green salad. I often make a double batch so that I've got leftovers for lunch the next day.

Ingredients

1 carton/can black beans, drained and rinsed
1 red or yellow pepper, diced
1 red chilli, finely chopped
2 spring onions, finely sliced
1 handful fresh coriander, finely chopped
Dressing
2 tbsp peanut or almond butter
1 lime, juiced
1 tsp miso
1 tsp cider vinegar
1 tsp maple syrup or raw honey

Instructions

Add the salad ingredients to a big bowl.
Mix the dressing ingredients and stir thoroughly.
Add to the salad and stir everything well together to combine.

Food as a way of connecting with family and community

For many people across the world, food is an important way of connecting with family, friends, and culture. The food we eat as adults can remind us of the meals we had with our families, or it can remind us of places we have lived and have connections with. Liz Pemberton, also known as the Black Nursery Manager, wrote an article for The Family Hub titled Taste of togetherness – food, culture, connection during Black History Month 2025, with a focus on food. In this article, she describes how sitting down to an African or Caribbean cuisine is an *immersive, full-body experience*. She also explains that the *food carries the weight of tradition, stories of migration and the essence of heritage.*

When I sit with friends from other places and experiences, and eat food that reminds them of home, there is something powerful in being introduced to something from their story through food.

My friend Albana lives in Yorkshire, but her family and home are in Albania. She shares her favourite recipe from home:

Albanian butterbean

Ingredients

500 g of dried butterbeans
1 onion
2 carrots
1 pepper
Some herbs and spices – I like a pinch of dried oregano and red chilli
2 tbsp of olive oil

Instructions

Fill a bowl with butter beans and cold water, leave to soak overnight.
The beans need a quick wash and drain.
Put the beans in a 2–3-litre pan
Cut the onion, carrot and peppers into four big pieces.
Add two spoons of olive oil, spices and herbs and the vegetables into the pot with the beans.
Boil for an hour in the slow cooker or on top of the oven.
If the beans seem dry, add some hot water and salt to cook for another 15 mins.
The taste is very unique, and most importantly, the dish is the best for your protein content.
Enjoy with bread or rice.

My friend Susan is from South Africa. There are two recipes she cooks regularly to remind her of home; these bring her comfort but also a joy in being able to share them with friends and her family.

Melk tart

Ingredients

For base

1 packet of rich tea or other plain biscuits
200g butter

Filling

3/4 of a cup or 93 g of plain flour and cornflour mix
4 cups or 944 ml of milk
3/4 cup or 125g sugar
3 eggs
1 tsp of vanilla paste
Pinch of salt
50 g of butter
Sprinkle of cinnamon

Instructions

Mix together crushed biscuits and butter for the pie base.
Press the mixture into a pie plate and refrigerate.
For the filling, mix together one cup of milk (236ml), the eggs, 50 g butter, vanilla, sugar, salt and the flour/cornflour mix.
Boil 3 cups of milk (708 ml).
Slowly add the flour/sugar/butter mix, stirring continuously until thickened.
Pour over the pie base and sprinkle the top with cinnamon.

Bobotie

Ingredients

2 slices of white bread
2 onions chopped

26 g butter
2 garlic cloves crushed
1 kg packet of lean minced beef
2 tbsp madras curry paste
1 tsp dried mixed herbs
3 cloves
5 allspice berries
2 tbsp peach or mango chutney
2.5 tbsp sultanas
6 bay leaves
For the topping:
300 ml full-fat milk
2 large eggs

Instructions

Heat oven to 180°C/350°F/Gas 4. Pour cold water over the bread and set aside to soak.
Meanwhile, fry the onions in the butter, stirring regularly for 10 mins until they are soft and starting to colour.
Add the garlic and beef and stir well, crushing the mince into fine grains until it changes colour.
Stir in the curry paste, herbs, spices, chutney, sultanas, and 2 of the bay leaves with 1 tsp salt and plenty of ground black pepper.
Cover and simmer for 10 mins.
Squeeze the water from the bread, then beat it into the meat mixture until well blended.
Tip into an oval ovenproof dish (23 x 33 cm and about 5–6 cm deep).
Press the mixture down well and smooth the top.
You can make this and chill one day ahead.

Jamel's thoughts on food

My comfort food is food that comes from my culture. Food like roti and curry chicken make me feel happy and connected to my family back in the Caribbean.

Did you know?

In 2003, UNESCO set up an Intangible Cultural Heritage of Humanity list. The aim is to protect and preserve social practices and food traditions. Some things included on this list are the Neapolitan pizza of Italy, the Baguette from France, Ceviche from Peru (raw fish marinated in lime) and the Mediterranean diet.

Food with others

Other people talk about food and the link to being with people to share the food with, and the comfort this brings.

Kathy's thoughts on food

Interestingly, when I think about feel-good foods, it's more about the preparation and being with people. Ian does a brilliant sourdough-based pizza, but it's as much about everyone in the kitchen, choosing their toppings, playing music and generally making a mess. Similarly, doing BBQs together or picking chillis from the greenhouse and then making a chilli together. Fish and chips/chips and gravy on the beach is probably the best though!!

In my interviews with people, some said food reminded them of places and memories:

Sarah's thoughts

I lived in Italy for a year, as part of the Erasmus course. My Italian neighbours taught me a very simple pasta recipe which is truly delicious and takes me right back to Pavia! I could honestly eat this every day.

Pasta recipe

Ingredients

300 g plain flour
2 eggs and 4 yolks (beaten)

Instructions

Put the ingredients in a food processor with a pinch of salt.
Knead the dough for 1 minute, wrap it in cling film and put it in the fridge for 30 minutes.
If you have a pasta machine, put through 1/4 of the dough at a time. If not, roll it very thin. Cut as required.
You can leave it to dry, but I am always too impatient and have to cook it immediately – it only takes a few minutes! Enjoy with a sauce made from fried garlic and onion added to tinned tomatoes, salt and pepper. Give the sauce a good blitz in the food processor. Top with grated parmesan.

Food as a source of nurture

In my role as a nurture worker with the children I support, I often use food in my sessions. I think sharing food with others can be an incredibly nurturing activity, and the children often love making food in our sessions. We often don't have access to cookers or kitchens, so I mostly do things that are simple and don't involve cooking. Just this week, we have been making edible sparklers (it was bonfire week), an easy, fun, nurturing activity that brought pure joy.

Edible sparklers

Ingredients

Bread sticks
Chocolate stars (you buy these in the baking section at the supermarket)
Icing pen
Sprinkles

Instructions

Put some icing on the back of the star and stick this on top of the bread stick.

Put more icing down a section of the bread stick and add sprinkles (I had sprinkles which included stars, balls and clouds).

Eat and enjoy!

Another favourite recipe, which a few of us use in the team from our colleague Sharon, is ginger biscuits. We often make these to take into school before Christmas, making them with Christmas cutters, and the children decorate them in our nurture session. Or if we work in a school with a kitchen we can use, we will bake them with the children.

Ginger biscuits

Ingredients

200 g plain flour
1/2 tsp of bicarbonate soda
1–2 tsp of ground ginger
2 tbsp of golden syrup
50 g margarine/ butter
75 g brown sugar.
1 egg

Instructions

Put all the ingredients into a bowl, apart from the syrup and water.

Rub these mixtures together until they look like breadcrumbs.

Add the syrup and water.

Mix the ingredients until they form a dough.

Knead the dough.

Roll and cut out.

Cook at 180°C/350°F/Gas 4 for 10 minutes. They will firm as you let them cool.

Another favourite is to make simple bread rolls. This does need kitchen facilities, but if you have one, it is a great sensory activity to do with children, and the kneading of the dough is a great stress reliever.

Bread rolls

Ingredients

340 g strong bread flour
1.5 tsp of quick yeast
1 tsp of sugar
A pinch of salt
1 tbsp of vegetable oil
220 ml of warm water

Instructions

Put the dry ingredients into a bowl and mix.
Add in the oil and water.
Start to mix together. When it starts to get sticky, put your hands in and knead the dough.
If it is too sticky, add a little more flour, or if it is too wet, add a little more water.
When it is all combined into a ball, take it out of the bowl and knead for around 5 minutes on a board.
Once it is kneaded, split it into 5 or 6 rolls.
You could make these into hedgehogs by pulling up spikes in the dough, or squash them a little and turn them into a face by adding raisins for the features.
Put them in a warm place and leave them to rise for an hour.
Bake in the oven for 25 minutes or until 200°C/400°F/Gas 6.

I also love how sharing food can be a way to show others that you care for and are thinking of them. Rachel, whom I mentioned above, really influenced and inspired me in this. For over 10 years, I worked with Rachel; we were friends before we started working together, and our children grew up with one another. Rachel is a foodie and an amazing cook. She taught my daughters to bake, which they loved (and I loved too, as she is a much more skilled baker than I am). She also showed me, through working with her, the joy she could bring to others in the workplace, of bringing in food and sharing it. I hadn't really seen this so much until I worked with her, and it is something I have taken with me. I now work in a peripatetic team, and we have team meetings roughly every six weeks where we get the chance to meet up. Sharing food has become a key part of our meetings. I often try to bring in something I have baked, and others in the team also do this. Twice a year, we meet together as a bigger team for a meal, where everyone brings something, often things they have made. Sharing food with friends and colleagues is nurturing and comforting. Below is one of the team's favourite recipes that I often make.

Tray bake macaroon

Ingredients

250 g white sugar
4 egg whites
300 g desiccated coconut
25 g gluten-free flour
Curd to add (I use curd recipes that I have included in Chapter 2)

Instructions

Mix the sugar and egg whites in a bowl.
Add the flour and coconut, and stir until they are combined.
Tip it into a lined tin (I use a small tin).
Dot curd into the mixture evenly.
Bake for around 30–40 minutes at 180°C/350°F/Gas 4.
It is baked when it is beginning to go brown around the edges.
Leave it for around 10 minutes to cool, and cut it into pieces without taking it out of the tin. It doesn't hold together brilliantly, but if you put it into the fridge, it will firm up.

Food for when we are feeling unwell

We all know that working with children can put us in contact with lots of viruses and bugs. Even if we eat well, stay hydrated and fit, we are going to inevitably pick up a virus, and at times like that we want food that is easy, nourishing and full of goodness. I have a few go-to recipes that we use as a family if any of us have a cold virus, and along with taking the elderberry liquor (I included the recipe in Chapter 2), these are the recipes that help get us through.

Butternut squash and apricot soup

Ingredients

1 tbsp of oil
1 butternut squash
1 onion
2 cloves of garlic
1 cm ginger, grated
Around 15 apricots
A pinch of salt
1 litre of vegetable stock

Instructions

Chop the onion and gently fry for a few minutes.
Add the crushed garlic and grated ginger.
Peel and chop the butternut squash into small pieces, add to the mixture and continue to gently fry.
Once this has all browned slightly, add the vegetable stock and apricots.
Allow to boil and then simmer until the squash is soft.
Blend together and serve.

Orange and pineapple smoothie

1 orange
1 pineapple (or a tin of pineapple in juice)
2 cm of ginger
1 teaspoon turmeric or 1 cm of fresh turmeric

Instructions

Peel the orange and add the segments of orange to the blender.
Peel the pineapple and add it to the blender.
Take the peel of the ginger, slice it and add it to the blender.
Peel the turmeric if using fresh, and add to the blender, or add the dried turmeric.
Blend everything together.
Either drink this as a smoothie or pour it into ice cube trays and add a few to a cup with hot water.

Lemon, honey, ginger cold relief

Ingredients

1 lemon
Runny honey
2 cm of ginger sliced
1 jam jar

Instructions

Add a few slices of honey to the bottom of the jam jar.
Add a few slices of ginger on top.
Cover with honey.
Repeat this until the lemon is covered.
Leave in the fridge, can be left for up to two weeks.
Add a few spoonfuls to a cup and pour boiling water over.
At night, add a tot of whisky and it's a perfect hot toddy!

Did you know?

Some of the foods suggested to eat when you're unwell are soup, garlic, lemon, ginger and honey; they all help with our immune function.

The joy from food

I believe that we can get joy from eating, maybe not all the time, but hopefully regularly. I know there are recipes I use that bring me joy. When I eat elderflower curd (see the recipe in Chapter 2), particularly the first batch of the year, it is a joyful experience; it tastes like early summer and feels full of hope. Another recipe which brings me joy is elderflower sorbet. Sharing these foods with others can increase the joyful experience.

Elderflower sorbet

Ingredients

100 g white sugar
500 ml water
250 ml of elderflower cordial

Instructions

Put the sugar and water in a saucepan and bring to the boil, stir until the sugar dissolves.
Take off the heat and stir in the cordial.
Chill it in the fridge for a few hours.
Churn it in an ice cream maker or pour it into a container, put it in the freezer, and stir every hour until frozen.

Moment for reflection

When you read the idea of joy from food, what is the food you think of?

Tasty treats

My youngest daughter suggested this section needed to be called tasty treats, as she believes these are essential for our wellbeing! I can't write a chapter on food without having recipes for cakes. I know we shouldn't eat these daily, but I also don't know an education-based staff room which doesn't rely on having some tasty treats to get them through the week. They can bring us comfort and joy.

Tamsin describes herself as having a sweet tooth and bakes regularly. Below is one of her cake recipes.

Banana bread

Ingredients

10 oz plain flour
1 tsp of baking powder
4 oz butter
8 oz caster sugar
2 eggs
4 ripe bananas (mash them)
3 floz of butter milk (or milk with 1 1/2 tsp of lemon juice)
1 teaspoon of vanilla extract

Instructions

Preheat the oven to 180°C/350°F/Gas 4.
Sift flour and baking powder in a bowl.
In a large bowl, cream butter and sugar together until light and fluffy.
Add eggs, mashed bananas, buttermilk and vanilla extract.
Mix well, and fold in flour.
Grease a 20 cm x 12.5 cm/ 8-inch by 5-inch tin.
Pour the mixture into the tin.
Bake for 55 min–1 hour.
Cool on a wire rack.

Fred works with me. He is gluten-free, and this is his favourite cake recipe

Sandwich cake

Ingredients

8 oz of gluten-free self-raising flour
8 oz of caster sugar
4 eggs
8 oz of butter/margarine
1/2 tsp of xanthan gum (add this to the flour)
1/2 tsp of vanilla essence (add this to the flour)

Instructions

Cream together the margarine and sugar.
Fold in 1/2 egg mix and 1/2 the flour and xanthan gum.
Repeat with the other half.
Grease and line two sandwich tins.
Pour the mixture into the tins.
Bake between 15–25 minutes at 170°C.
Leave to cool, then add jam and sandwich together.

Did you know?

Icing used to be spread on cakes with a feather, and before the whisk was invented, people used to whisk egg whites with a bundle of twigs.

Conclusion

This chapter is full of recipes; I hope they have inspired you to try something new. I think there is something incredibly nurturing in the act of sharing a recipe. I love asking people for recipes and sharing recipes I have. This year, I have bought myself and my daughters a blank recipe book each, to fill in with the recipes we each love. I have added recipes that they have shared with me, and I know they will have recipes that I often make too.

Ideas on how to incorporate this into early years practice and at home

- Make a recipe book at home or in the setting of your favourite recipes. You could use a blank notebook or print out recipes you like, involving the children and families in this.
- Regularly make food with children, maybe they could make their lunch once a week.
- Find out from the families you work with about their favourite recipes. Can you use some of these in the setting?
- Try different foods with the children, maybe try and introduce a new food to try each week or month, this might be fruit and vegetables that are in season, or food from around the world, or different colours of fruit and vegetables.
- If you grow vegetables or fruit in the nursery/school garden or in the house, bring them in so you can all try eating them.

If you have

If you have 2 minutes, eat some nuts and a few berries. Eat them slowly and notice the flavours and textures.

If you had 10 minutes, you could try making Chris's black bean salad recipe, adjust the recipe to fit with what you have in your fridge.

If you had 20 minutes, you could try making one of the soup recipes, think about the number of plant-based foods you are able to add to the soup.

If you had 40 minutes, you could try baking one of the cake or traybake recipes; you might like to make this to share with family, friends or colleagues.

References

BBC fermented food: https://www.bbc.co.uk/food/articles/fermented_foods

British Heart Foundation: https://www.bhf.org.uk/informationsupport/heart-matters-magazine/news/behind-the-headlines/ultra-processed-foods

British Heart Foundation: Eating on a Budget: https://www.bhf.org.uk/informationsupport/heart-matters-magazine/nutrition/eat-well-on-a-budget

Greenbelt Jack Munro interview: https://www.greenbelt.org.uk/talks/in-conversation-with-jack-monroe/

Jack Munro blog: https://oursouthend.wordpress.com/

Mental Health Foundation: https://www.mentalhealth.org.uk/explore-mental-health/a-z-topics/diet-and-mental-health

NHS: The Eatwell Guide: https://www.nhs.uk/live-well/eat-well/food-guidelines-and-food-labels/the-eatwell-guide/

Olio: https://olioapp.com/en/

Taste of togetherness food, culture, connection: https://nfamilyclub.com/parenting/taste-of-togetherness-food-culture-and-connection/

YouGov: https://yougov.co.uk/society/articles/43386-how-confident-are-britons-kitchen?redirect_from=/topics/society/articles-reports/2022/08/10/how-confident-are-britons-kitchen

Zoe: https://zoe.com/learn/30-plants-per-week

5 Creativity and culture

During the COVID lockdown many people took the opportunity to engage in more creative activities. For some, this was rediscovering old hobbies, and for others it was a chance to try new things. For some people, this just lasted through that very strange, specific time, but I know for others it is something they have continued to explore and develop. Many people found the act of engaging in a creative process supported their wellbeing; for others, it also gave them an unexpected boost of joy.

I am married to an artist, Iain, who is a letter cutter and carver. I know I am biased, but his work is beautiful, and our house is full of his art and the art of many of our friends. We are so fortunate that many of our friends are musicians, sculptors, potters, printers, painters, writers and poets, so in our small world, engaging in creative acts is seen as normal. But maybe that's not your world, and maybe the idea of spending time doing something creative is possibly a bit out of your comfort zone. I am hoping in this chapter to share some ideas around being creative, and maybe there will be some things that you might think you would like to try. As in other chapters, I am going to pull in other voices on how they use creativity to support their wellbeing.

Moment for reflection

Just for a moment, think about the last time you engaged in a creative process, it may be cooking something new, playing an instrument, painting, knitting or sewing. It doesn't matter what it was, but try to recall when you last did something creative and how it made you feel.

DOI: 10.4324/9781003717591-6

Creativity and wellbeing

There is growing research into how creativity can support our wellbeing and mental health. An organisation called The What Works Wellbeing, a research community exploring what supports adults' wellbeing, created a project with the University of Arts London from September 2023 to January 2024. One of the questions they were asking was: *What are the effects of creativity and creative participation on personal wellbeing?* As part of this study, they looked at 16,434 studies. The studies looked at creative activities in the UK, the Republic of Ireland, Lithuania, Germany, Spain, the Netherlands, Hungary, Finland, Turkey, the USA, Canada, New Zealand, Australia and Hong Kong. The studies were in a range of settings from community venues, colleges, universities, hospitals and medical schools, a prison, an arts centre and a WhatsApp group. The creative activities were varied and included writing, video work, theatre, clay, drawing and art therapy, to list a few. The people attending were a wide range of ages, mostly women and mostly white. There are clearly limitations with this study, but it did show how creative interventions can positively affect a range of wellbeing outcomes. From their study, they found that it had particularly positive outcomes with:

- Quality of life and social connectedness for young people with diagnosed mental health conditions
- Quality of life for patients with Dementia, Alzheimer's and breast cancer
- Mental wellbeing for healthcare professionals
- Isolation, depression and mental ill health for older people
- Improved mood and reduced anxiety among young adults, pregnant women and prisoners

Mental Health UK have a useful article about how creativity can improve mental health. They recognise that it is not always the first thing we think of for practising self-care and that when we are busy, it can feel hard to incorporate creative practice into our routine. It is easy to think creativity is about having a perfect end result, but just in the way we talk about the value of creativity being about the process with children and not the finished product, it is the experience of the doing, not what it looks like at the end, that is the same for us. Engaging in creative practices engages our brain, especially our subconscious, and through this, it can be hugely helpful in supporting our mental health and emotions. Being involved in creative activities has been shown to decrease depression and anxiety, and burnout, and it can boost our immune system.

In 2019, the World Health Organization produced a research paper looking at *what is the evidence on the role of the arts in improving health and wellbeing*. They looked at 3000 studies and found evidence that involvement in the arts can potentially help both mental and physical health. They looked at two areas:

Prevention and promotion

In this category, they found that the arts can:

- Can affect the social determinants of health
- Support child development
- Encourage health-promoting behaviours
- Help to prevent ill health
- Support caregiving

Management and treatment

In this category, they found:

- It helps people who are experiencing mental illness
- It supports people with acute conditions
- It supports people with neurodevelopmental and neurological conditions
- It assists with the management of noncommunicable diseases
- It supports end-of-life care

There is an article on the BBC culture web page exploring why creativity is good for us. It starts with a quote from the wonderful author Maya Angelou (she is one of my favourite authors), who describes creativity as a bottomless pit: *"the more you use it, the more you have it"*. I know for some the idea of being creative feels quite alien, particularly if their experience of creative subjects at school was a negative experience. I am interested in how our early experiences of creativity can go on to influence our engagement as adults. In 2023, I wrote a book, *Creativity and wellbeing in the*

Early Years, where I explored how we can support children's wellbeing through a wide range of creative experiences. I mostly had a negative experience of creativity at school; I couldn't draw or paint, I am not very musical and I left school feeling that creativity was not for me. It was through being married to Iain that I learned creativity is for everyone; everyone can engage in creative acts, it's about finding the right one for you, and giving ourselves permission to try and have a go. I still can't draw or paint, but I do knit and sew and sometimes crochet. I have discovered a love of printing, and I adore making balms, salves and soaps, and I enjoy cooking. They are just different forms of being creative from those that I heard about at school.

Building our resilience

The National Gallery's website suggests that art should be a safe space, a place where we can experiment, take risks, fail at things and try again. They suggest that through these acts we build resilience, through the process of experimenting, playing and retrying, and that these processes can help us to deal with uncertainty.

I firmly believe that if we want children to engage in creative acts, we need to have a willingness to have a go ourselves, modelling the trying and engaging. This is particularly relevant to those children who are a bit anxious or unsure about trying something creative.

Moment for reflection

Do you talk to and, if possible, share the creative things you do with the children you work with?

In this next section, I am going to explore a range of various creative activities, similar to other chapters, which will include a variety of voices from people who engage in different creative forms.

Using clay

I use a lot of creative activities with the children I support, and mostly they are open-ended, so I provide the material and the children can create what they like. I discovered a few years ago how brilliant clay is for supporting children's wellbeing. I have worked with an artist called Clare Day, who is a ceramicist and runs workshops for children and adults to discover the joy of making with clay. In my book *Creativity and wellbeing* (2023), I interviewed Clare, and she describes why she likes using clay with children: *"What I love with clay is it gives you the chance to do something again and again and again and then squash it up"*. This has been my experience with children. I have found that many children love the ability to make something with the clay without it being too difficult. It holds better than playdough; they can keep it if they want to, but they often love repeatedly restarting with it. There is also something about the sensory appeal of clay that attracts many children. I have seen very agitated children become so much calmer when they play with clay.

Earlier this year, I went on a wellbeing workshop facilitated by Clare, run at Bath Spa University, where she works. The session was using clay and natural resources. It was an experiential workshop, giving us the opportunity for 2.5 hours to play, make, create and experiment. We were sitting under a willow tree by the river, using natural resources around us such as leaves, twigs, grass and also natural materials Clare had brought to use in printing on the clay. This was such a relaxing session; it was term 6, which is always a crazy term for me. There was something incredibly nurturing about taking the morning to be creative and play with clay. I am good at supporting my wellbeing, and I go through stages of being very creative, but there was something about intentionally doing a workshop where the focus was on playing, experimenting, rather than making the end product that I found incredibly liberating and nurturing.

I always thought you needed a kiln to use real clay, but I discovered through Clare that you can let it air dry. You can buy clay from potter suppliers, and it's not that expensive. Our local suppliers sell a large bag of clay, around 12 kg, for less than £10. Other options are air-dry clay, which has a lot of plastic in it. I am less keen on using it for this reason, but I have recently been experimenting with making air-dry clay. This feels different from real clay, but it is a less messy alternative and does feel like the air-dry clay you can buy.

A recipe is below:

Air dry clay

2 cups of bicarbonate soda
1 cup of cornflour
1 1/2 cups of water

Instructions

Put all the ingredients in a pan and keep stirring until they bind together like dough. It won't be fully formed, but it sticks to the spoon and itself mostly.

Let the clay cool, then put it onto a hard surface and knead it with more cornflour. You will need around another three cups of cornflour, but add some at a time and keep kneading until it stops being sticky and holds together.

Use it as you would shop bought air dry clay, it's particularly good for cutting shapes in. This year, the children I work with made Christmas decorations with cutters out of the clay.

It lasts in an air-tight container for around two weeks.

It takes around four days to dry (depending on how warm the room is).

If clay is something you like the idea of trying, I would recommend going to a workshop. I have done a few, and they are a lot of fun and very calming. Many cities now have clay workshops as day events that people can try out as a taster session; these are often run by local potters. In Bath, there are a few different clay studios. There is also a website called Yuup, which advertises craft workshops in a few different cities in the UK. Currently, it covers Bath, Bristol, Cardiff, Nottingham, Birmingham, Brighton & Hove, Southampton and Durham, but I think they are looking to grow.

Did you know?

There is evidence from 2500 BC that clay was used for medicinal purposes to treat wounds and prevent haemorrhages.

Knitting and crochet

A growing number of people turn to knitting and crocheting as their favoured wellbeing creative activity. I wonder if Tom Daly has possibly increased its popularity. I knit, but on a fairly basic level, and I tend to have phases of knitting. I have knitted quite a few resources to use with the children I support, including a set of colour monsters and a bear. I have tried crocheting and had a little success, but I don't find it as easy as knitting. I am interested in how a growing number of young people are taking up crocheting and knitting. Many of my daughter's friends knit and crochet. My eldest daughter lives in Norway, where knitting is a popular activity. Eighteen months ago, she joined a knitting group of women her age and learned to knit. Her knitting ability has surpassed my ability already. Last Christmas, she knitted me fingerless gloves with an owl on them, which she designed herself; she clearly has inherited her father's creative genes! But when I do knit, and it works, I find it incredibly rewarding and satisfying, although there have been projects that have been a bit of a disaster.

Most research on creativity and wellbeing has been focused on arts such as drawing and music. In 2020, there was some research conducted by Dr Pippa Burns and Dr Rosemary Van Der Meer from the University of Wollongong. The paper is titled "Happy Hookers- Findings from an international study exploring the effects of crochet on wellbeing". They had 8,391 people take part in an online survey about crocheting: 99.1% of the respondents were female, aged between 41–60, living in 87 different countries. The majority of the respondents said that crocheting made them feel calmer and happier, and they experienced significant improvement in their mood after crocheting. They concluded that crocheting can offer positive benefits to wellbeing with many respondents saying they used to support themselves through times of chronic pain, grief and to help manage mental health conditions.

My colleague Sharon is a keen crocheter. She describes how it supports her wellbeing.

Sharon and crochet

One of the wellbeing activities I most enjoy is crocheting. Choosing a project and the process of selecting yarn are an important part of the process for me. If I am starting a blanket project, I like to use yarn which works easily and doesn't "catch" on your hook. This type of crochet I can do while chatting, watching TV, and it is so relaxing and satisfying and doesn't require a great deal of concentration. The project grows very quickly, which helps me feel I have achieved something special while enjoying something I enjoy doing.

The other type of crochet, when making an animal toy as a present, requires following a pattern and knowing exactly where I am in the process. This type of crochet helps my brain to totally focus on the next step, counting every stitch. The focus and concentration, coupled with the joy of making something for someone I love, helps me feel relaxed and at peace. I can switch my brain off from all the busy thoughts of the day and get into my stitch rhythm. I can feel this relaxing my body and mind as I sit and become completely absorbed by it.

The pleasure I get from completing a project and wrapping it ready to gift to someone adds to my sense of wellbeing. I feel my creation represents time and something of myself, which shows my love and care for the person I am gifting it to. So, from selecting yarn to wrapping and gifting, crochet is a great way to boost my wellbeing, relaxation and feel-good endorphins.

If crocheting or knitting is something you would like to learn, there are loads of online videos to help you. I recommend the LoveCraft website, which sells everything you need to start with knitting and crocheting and also has some tutorial videos and patterns for free. A great website for finding numerous free patterns is Ravelry.

A simple way to start with crochet or knitting is making a dishcloth, using 100% cotton yarn. These are quick to make. Below is how I knit them.

Dishcloth pattern

Knitting needles size 6
Cast on 40 stitches
Knit a row
Then continue to knit each row until you have the size of the dishcloth you want
Cast off

Did you know?

There is evidence of knitting as we know it dating back to 500 AD in Egypt and the Middle East

Sewing

For this book, I have gathered lots of ideas from people across early years and education. One of the people who responded is Laura, who lives on the Isle of Man. She shared her love of sewing.

Laura and sewing

My main thing is sewing! I was attending a class every Tuesday, which meant I stopped working at 3 pm and went to my class until 6 pm. It was so lovely that I went with my friend and got to know two other people, plus our instructor. I didn't take my phone with me and completely switched off.

From this sewing class, I then converted one of my daughter's bedrooms into a sewing room (she had moved to the UK!) I have my own little haven.

I enjoy creating for others, purses, toiletry bags, and anything else that takes my fancy! I've even set up an Instagram page!

Sunday nights used to be my time to go into my sewing room.

The sewing class disbanded; however, I still sew whenever I can.

At Christmas, I also took up knitting! This is tricky, but it means that I can sit in the lounge with my husband and knit. My sewing room is great when he has rugby to watch!

Knitting doesn't come naturally at all, but I find that it really fills my bucket!

Another thing I do is doodle! I look on TikTok for ideas and go from there. This is more of a travel go-to as taking my sewing or knitting away is a bit awkward!

I was always crafty when I was a child, and coming back to it in later life has really helped my wellbeing.

I have to concentrate so hard on what I'm doing, I can't think of anything else! When sewing, I usually have something on Netflix on my iPad. I'm not really watching it, but listening to it! Virgin River was great for this! Emily in Paris is not so good when they were talking in French, and I don't speak French!

Getting started with sewing

If sewing is something you would like to try, there are a few options:

Sewing with a machine
Hand sewing
Embroidery
Cross-stitch and Needlepoint (these two are variations on embroidery)

Hand sewing and embroidery are two different techniques where you are using a needle and thread. Hand sewing is where you need to join pieces of fabric together, and embroidery is used to decorate fabric. The great advantage of hand sewing and embroidery is that you have minimal kit; a sewing machine is great, but takes up room, and they are not cheap. Whereas hand sewing can be as simple as some thread, needles and material.

As Laura describes above, you can find a class in your area or take online tutorials.

Spruce Crafts website has a useful online beginner's guide to hand sewing with the basics of how to thread a needle and some basic stitches. They also have a beginner's guide to embroidery and cross-stitch with guidance on what you need to get started. If you want to learn how to use a sewing machine, the website Prima has a useful starter guide.

Using sewing with children

In the last year, I have used sewing with a few children I worked with. I had a feeling that it might be something that brought them some calm. I bought some basic sewing kits from Hobbycraft. There was one little girl, and it was absolutely the right creative activity to share with her; she was having an incredibly hard day, and she had just heard some devastating news. The sewing enabled her to focus on something totally different; we did it together; it was slow, it was repetitive, and it was incredibly calming. It was really moving to see how impactful it was in that moment for her.

I sew, it's one of the few GCSEs I achieved! I don't do it a lot anymore. When my girls were little, I did a lot of cross-stitch and made book character badges in cross-stitch to sew onto their clothes. A few weeks ago, I decided to start sewing again, so I bought a small tapestry kit. I have started using it when I get home from work, listening to an audiobook and sewing. I have found it's a good way to help me switch off, and it doesn't require too much headspace.

Drawing

This is something I am not in a position to talk about. I have a deep mistrust of myself and drawing. I can link it back to being told as a 4-year-old that I couldn't show my picture in a school assembly as it wasn't good enough! I would like to learn to draw, and I have talked about it for a few years, but I haven't yet been quite brave enough to properly try. I have tinkered, but always feel deeply embarrassed by my effort, but it is on my creative bucket list to conquer!

The director of the team I work for used to be the head of a nursery and then head of an infant school, before moving to our team. Ed has developed a practice of daily drawing. I love this dedication and commitment he has. Below, he describes how drawing supports his wellbeing. I suspect when he was headteacher this was particularly crucial for him.

Ed on drawing

I do a drawing every day, and always "from life", looking at something in front of me, translating 3D to 2D, not copying a drawing or photograph. It doesn't matter how meagre the drawing is, in fact, the very fast ones are often the best! The book that got me started is The Creative License *by Danny Gregory. He continually challenges you to start drawing, now, at once . . . what are you waiting for? It's funny, energetic, accessible and inspiring.*

It's something I've been doing for 14 years so far, and it's the every-day aspect of my sketching habit that's most important to me. The sketches might be small or large, hurried or methodical, incomplete or highly finished, the key thing is that I have really looked at some part of life that day and described it on the page. Over the years, this regular habit of observing and translating the world into pictures has given me a past time that is richly rewarding.

I love the way that sketching is mostly analogue rather than digital. It is very rooted in touch and sight; ink drying on the paper, colours mixing in the palette, the movement of the brush or pencil across the page.

It's cheap; after the initial outlay on a pencil and a sketchbook, it just costs time (and the patience of those around you . . .).

I like the way that it is largely non-verbal; even a familiar group of people sketching together are mostly silent, absorbed in the practice of their art. Paradoxically, it's also very sociable, from fellow sketchers sharing ideas and pictures, to strangers intrigued by what you are drawing.

And I love the way that it serves no practical purpose other than to gratify; it is an excellent provider of "flow", the wonderful feeling of unself-conscious engagement that comes when you are totally absorbed in task that is challenging, but well matched to your abilities (I highly recommend reading The Happiness Hypothesis *by Jonathan Haidt, especially Chapter 5, for more on "flow"). You get direct feedback from the page on how well you are doing, and improvement is visible, given time . . . whenever you can find the time, as long as it's regular, hopefully daily.*

If learning to draw is something you like the idea of trying, there is a useful guidance sheet and video on the City Lit website. Many cities will have drawing classes you can attend; some of these will be for beginners. A quick Google search of your area will let you know what is available.

Colouring in

If drawing is not your thing, you may like to try colouring in. I know many people who find this activity incredibly calming. There is a growing market in colouring books for adults, with a range of pictures or patterns to use. Often with colouring in it's less about the end product but more about the experience of doing.

Printing

Over the last few years, I have been experimenting with printing with the children I work with. My husband suggested it while I was writing the book on creativity for children, and I have become quite hooked on it. It works brilliantly for children, but I also love it for myself. Below, I am going to describe a few ways I use printing, both with children and for myself.

Printing with ink and natural materials

For this, you need

Ink
Rollers
Hard surface to roll on
Natural materials such as leaves, flowers, bark
Card/ paper/material to print on
Squeeze some ink onto a smooth surface
Roll it out until the ink is smooth
Roll the ink onto the object, such as a leaf
Put paper on top of the object
Rub the back of the paper with a clean roller
Peel off the paper and see the print of the object
You can print on paper, card and on material.

Hapa Zome printing

Another form of printing that I often do with children is flower bashing, its real name is Hapa Zome, this is a Japanese practice.

For this, you need

Flowers
Leaves
Material
Hammer or pebble
Paper

Place your flowers and leaves onto the material, cover them with paper and then repeatedly hit the flowers and leaves. Once you start to see colour coming through, lift off the paper and flowers and enjoy the prints on the material. This is such a satisfying creative outlet, especially if you're feeling stressed; it's hugely releasing and satisfying.

Flowers that work well for this are:

Violas
Calendulas
Hollyhocks
Geraniums
Cosmos
Dandelions
Dandelion leaves
Plantain leaves
Sage leaves

When I do this activity with children, it brings such joy to them; they love being allowed to hit something, and they are always utterly delighted when they see the prints. Every time, the children have been thrilled to see what they have created.

Printing with stamps

Another, simpler way of printing is using ink and stamps, and using this to decorate paper, which you can use for wrapping. You can buy stamps and ink from many different places. I like the Indian Block Print company; they sell stamps (although they describe them as blocks), which they have made in India, where they work with carvers to carve the blocks. You press each block into ink or paint and press this onto material or paper. I often use these with children to decorate a bag at the end of the school year, and I have decorated tea towels and bags as presents for friends. I think printing with stamps is one of those creative activities you can do without needing to be very creative. It is quick to do and very satisfying.

Writing

Some people find writing is a massive boost to their wellbeing, and the process of putting down their thoughts on paper can be a helpful way to get them out of their head. The Radio 4 program Women's Hour has a page on its website and an interview with psychotherapist Julia Samuel, where she explores how writing can be therapeutic. She talks about journaling as a process for writing down your thoughts, using this as a stream of consciousness, where your focus is on the getting the thoughts out of your head and not worrying about what it looks like (the spelling/grammar etc.). Her suggestion is to do this first thing in the morning. She also suggests that writing can change the messages in our heads.

Obviously, I write. For me, writing is more about the enjoyment of the creative process rather than trying to sort out what's in my head. Although sometimes when I am in the middle of writing a book and struggling, it doesn't always feel like enjoyment! I never saw myself as a writer. I have several dyslexia traits. My grammar is appalling, and I was often made to feel in previous jobs that my writing was poor. I initially started writing a blog as a creative way to process my nurture work with children. I was approached and asked if I would write a book for the publishers Jessica Kingsley Publishers in 2016. To be honest, I thought the initial email was spam and almost deleted it. My first book was published in 2017. Over the last 10 years, I have realised I love writing, I find the practice of putting words onto paper quite soothing. Although I am often writing about the direct work I do with children, I find the experience of writing about it meets a creative desire. Over the years, I have developed my own rituals and practices around writing. I am fortunate in that I can sit and write anywhere, but my preference is writing with a view. I have an office at the bottom of my garden, and my desk is in front of the large window looking over my garden, but this is my summer space as mice visit it in the winter, and I am terrified of mice! My winter writing space is often at the end of my dining-room table, on my day off, or first thing in the morning. From here, I look out through the dining-room window, and I can see the bench with pots of plants outside the back door and bird feeders. When I read back over some of my books, I often mention where I wrote a section, and as I read it back, I can vividly see myself in that place. There is a cottage we often rent out in Cornwall which overlooks the sea. That is my favourite spot. The next time I am there, I will have finished this book. But I think I will probably find some writing to do. I mostly write in silence, but if I do listen to music, there are only two musicians I can have on, and that is Olafur Arnalds and Max Richter.

I have been asked several times how to get into writing and how to find the time. My tips are:

Just start!
Don't think too hard, sit and write
Don't edit to start with, just write what is in your mind, editing is for later
Try to make it a regular practice, find a regular time that works for you
Find a writing place that works for you
Be kind to yourself, don't berate your work
Don't worry about the number of words or the amount of time, just sit, write, practice; even if it is only 20 words in 20 minutes, that is ok.

One of my good friends is a poet, and she describes her experience of writing and performing poetry.

Jo on poetry

Both reading and writing poetry are, for me, essential tools for my well-being. When you work in stressful and challenging circumstances, poetry sometimes is the only language that can resonate with what you're feeling and experiencing. It somehow goes deeper than more overtly descriptive writing. There have been so many times I've read a poem and been deeply moved, recognising that a poet had perfectly captured something I was going through or feeling. Those moments made me feel less alone as I realised others felt this way too! I also benefit from the short form of poetry – I don't always have time to read a book, so dipping in and out of a poetry book when I have a few moments is perfect for me.

Writing and performing poetry has also helped me vent, express my feelings, release emotion from my body, process and make sense of things I have experienced. Nothing holds space quite like a blank page! If I'm really honest I can sometimes find it difficult how bad people are at listening – I find that so many colleagues or friends I talk to, rather than being curious or asking questions, can (I recognise with the best of intentions!) offer unwanted advice, skip to finding a "fix", give partially relevant anecdotes or even flip the conversation back to them which really isn't what I need in the moment! A blank page is the best of listeners – it can be a friend that just listens, absorbs difficult things, holds it all and keeps it safe for you.

If writing is something you would like to have a go at, but you're not sure where to start, there are a few ideas below:

Try journaling- writing down your reflections on your day/week.
Try writing something creative; it might be a short story.
You might want to look out of the window for inspiration, write about what you see, and how it makes you feel.

You might like to try writing a poem, or you could try a Haiku. This is an unrhymed three-line poem; it is based on the traditional Japanese poetic form. The most common way to write this in English is to write the first and last line with five syllables and the middle line with seven syllables.

Singing

There is growing recognition of the impact singing can have on wellbeing. Jacques Launay wrote an article for the University of Oxford Research page, exploring how singing can boost wellbeing. It is recognised that singing is good for improving breathing, posture and muscle tension; it's also recognised that it can help in pain relief, due to the release of endorphins (similar to when we exercise), and it can reduce the stress hormone cortisol. Michael Mosley looked at singing for his series, "Just one thing"; he explored how singing can release "happy hormones" such as dopamine and endorphins, which can give us a natural high. He also found some research that suggested singing can have similar effects to cannabis. Apparently, endocannabinoids are a recently discovered set of chemical compounds that are naturally found in the body. They have a similar action to the active part of cannabis. Other studies have also shown that singing in a group for just one hour can boost your immune system, and it can help to reduce inflammation. Lower levels of inflammation help our immune system to fight against infections, but inflammation is also linked with our mental health. Some GPs are now referring patients to a choir to support their mental health.

On the back of reading this piece, we had a team WhatsApp conversation about it. Kate, one of my colleagues, has a nine-year-old son, Luca, who adores singing and is in a choir. She said when he was little, he would often go to sleep singing a song to himself and then wake up and carry on where he had left the song; it was as if he had just pressed pause. I love the way children will often show us how happy they are by singing to themselves. She also told us that her husband Nitin has a stammer, and discovered when it first developed that he could sing without stammering.

Charlie is one of my oldest friends. She is now in Malaysia, where she is head of RE at an international school. Singing has been such an important part of her wellbeing for years; she describes below how it makes her feel.

Charlie on singing

Singing has always been a place of solace, where everything fades away, and only the music remains. There's no greater feeling than a band rehearsal, trying out new harmonies or ad-libbing a riff, where part of me relaxes into just letting go. To close my eyes and feel something inside become tangible, an emotional release like no other.

Whether I'm with the band, belting out songs in the car or on stage with a choir, my mood instantly improves, and there's often a bond with others too. Singing and creating music together, doing something that we all love, is an act of connection that feeds my soul.

Fred is one of my colleagues, he sings in a male voice choir and describes how important it is for him.

Fred on singing

I've been singing in a choir for almost 20 years, and on a personal level, it enriches my life in several ways. Firstly, I love the feeling of singing. I feel strong, and I feel confident. Secondly, I love the community of singers I meet with every week; the friendships and care that come from those relationships are very important to me. I feel connected to something much bigger. And lastly, I love the feeling of performing in front of an audience. People have smiled, people have cried, and people have joined in with joy at concerts. Connecting with myself, my body and connecting with others brings light into my life.

I know many people who feel that singing really boosts their wellbeing, and several of my friends are in choirs. In 2024, the University of the West of England and a music venue called St George's led a research project called Sing for Happiness. Participants took part in choir sessions and data from 361 people was collected on their mood. The research found their mood was immediately improved by singing together, and the participants talked about feeling calmer, happier and more energised.

If singing with others is something you like the idea of being involved in, there is a website called Natural Voice Network, where you put in your postcode, and it will tell you of singing groups in your area.

Did you know?

Our voices are as unique as a fingerprint. No two voices are identical

Photography

Most of us have cameras as part of our phones, and many of us use them often to capture moments of joy, times with family and friends, or to remember experiences. Taking photos can be a creative activity. The joy of the camera on our phones is that they have vastly improved and can take decent images, without us having to be excellent photographers. I have a friend who is a therapist, and for a while, he worked on a mindful project where he photographed something each day that caught his attention. He had no rules other than to notice and capture it in a photograph.

Moment for reflection

Take a moment to think about a creative project you might like to try, maybe do some research on how you could do this, or write yourself a reminder that you would like to try it.

Engaging in culture

This next section is going to explore how creativity can boost our well-being without us directly doing a creative activity. I am aware that, for some, the idea of having the headspace, time and energy to actively start doing something creative feels far too much. But there are other ways that creativity can boost us, and that is through watching/listening/looking, by listening to music, watching a film or a play, or looking at a painting.

In 2025, King's College London launched a research project measuring the physiological responses of participants while viewing masterpieces by world-renowned artists, including Van Gogh and Manet. This study was co-funded by the Art Fund and the Psychiatry Research Trust. The research found that viewing art activates the immune, hormone and autonomic nervous systems all at once. Apparently, this has never been recorded before. This was a small study, with just 50 participants aged 18–40, who were monitored for heart rate variability and skin temperature using research digital watches to track the participants' levels of interest and arousal. They also measured cortisol levels through saliva samples, which show stress levels. They found that cortisol levels fell by 22%, and participants also showed psychological signs of excitement. The gallery they used for this research was The Courtauld in London; it's one of my favourite galleries. It isn't too big, it's curated really well and it has pieces by artists such as Monet, Manet and Van Gogh, and a stunning collection of medieval art. I have been twice this year, and each time I stood in front of a painting titled Antibes, by Claude Monet (if you go to their website and put the title in their collection, you will see an image of the painting). Both times I have been moved to tears by this painting. I am not sure I can fully explain why, but I do know it feels incredibly calming. It's a painting of a tree over the sea, and the sea is so inviting; maybe it reminds me of moments of pure joy and peacefulness of being in water, but also, I know on those visits I have been feeling quite stressed (I love visiting London, but I always find it stressful). I think the painting reminded me of calm times and places.

Some galleries we need to pay to visit, but many are free. Many cities have free museums and galleries. Galleries and museums work hard at making their spaces accessible, often offering guidance notes on what you are seeing, with some hints or tips on what to look for. The Tate website has a useful page with tips on how to look slowly at art, seeing it as a mindful practice. They recognise that art galleries and museums can feel overwhelming, with so much work to see. Their suggestion is to engage in slow looking, where you choose a piece of artwork and stand or sit in front of it for five minutes or more. Their tips are:

- Make yourself comfortable in front of the artwork.
- Don't worry if nothing comes to mind at first; try to forget any expectations. Keep an open mind.
- Pay attention to your first impressions.
- Let your eyes wander and see what connections you make; it doesn't matter if the artist intended these or not. It is about what you see.
- Be aware of your surroundings. It's ok to be distracted by what is going on around you.
- Pay attention to how you feel looking at the art piece.

Visiting galleries as a family

We took our daughters to galleries from the time they were babies, and continue to visit galleries as a family when we are together. Sometimes, you can worry that a gallery is not a place for a child, but many galleries now actively want to engage families. I love seeing the different ways galleries do this. The Tate galleries are particularly good at this; each of the Tate galleries has free booklets and pencils for children to use as they go around, with suggestions of pieces of art to look for and ways to respond to the artwork. I love seeing children sitting in front of a piece of art, sketching what they see. The Tate galleries run many free workshops for families, especially during holiday times. The Tate website family pages state: *"Welcome to Tate! Make noise in our galleries. After you've enjoyed some art, there are plenty of places to stop and eat or have a break, and you can breastfeed wherever you like. Buggies are always welcome."* I think this is a wonderful, encouraging and inclusive statement. Jamel Campbell has run play sessions for babies and families at the V&A and story sessions for families at Tate Britain. If you have young children and can get to one of these, I think they would be delightful.

How to engage children in art

- Don't worry about seeing everything!
- See if the gallery has a children's guide.
- When you arrive, see if there is anything listed that your children like the sound of; there might be an artist they have heard of.
- Wander and see what catches their eye.
- Look at a piece together, what do they notice? Ask a few gentle questions, for example: I wonder why . . ., I wonder what . . ., what can you see . . ., how does it make you feel . . ., do you think there is a story about this piece?
- You might decide to look for a theme, maybe finding the pictures with the most shapes in, or the most naked people, or the cutest babies, or animals that you like.

Some exhibitions are aimed specifically at families, such as Lost Spells, an exhibition of Jackie Morris paintings based on the book she and Robert Macfarlane wrote. This is a travelling exhibition. It was in the Victoria Gallery in Bath over the summer of 2025. Jackie's paintings are stunning. If you are not familiar with her work, look at the Lost Words website. The exhibition is one of the most family-friendly curated exhibitions I have seen. Alongside the beautiful paintings of animals and birds, there are spell poems written by Robert, also dressing-up clothes, a tree to hide in, a reading corner and art activities. In the feedback book at the Victoria art gallery, I noticed a comment saying there were too many children in the gallery! I took this to be a wonderful endorsement of how successful this show was. I visited it several times, and it was always full of families engaging, having fun and enjoying the space.

How to find a gallery

Most cities have an art gallery; many of these are free to visit. There are several Tates across the country, with two in London, one in St Ives (this one charges) and one in Liverpool; these are always worth visiting. If you would like to know what galleries are in an area, the Art Fund website has a useful explore page. Put in a postcode or the name of an area, and it will list for you the art galleries and museums in that area.

The joy of experiencing art

As I have mentioned, I really enjoy seeing art and going to galleries. But I particularly like seeing art in nature and in unexpected places. There is an artist called Luke Jerram who is multi-disciplinary artist, and some of the pieces he has made are Helios (the sun), The Moon and Gaia (the Earth). These are huge sculptures of the moon, sun, and earth. They are often exhibited in cathedrals, national trust buildings and sometimes outside. We saw Gaia outside in a wooded grove at Greenbelt Festival one year, and recently we had the opportunity to see Helios in a swimming pool in Bristol! There was something incredible about swimming under a magnificent sculpture. It made me realise that the combination of art and swimming is such a joyful and brilliant experience for me; if I were able to add being outside, that would make it perfect! I think I will do some research to see if that is available.

Kerry told me about her experience of visiting galleries and experiencing art, which I found really moving.

I grew up in a lower-working-class household and the idea of going to a museum, exhibition or art gallery was really out of reach. I thought it was just for posh people. But I had a great aunt who introduced me to art and taught me that the way we engage creatively is unique, and I needed to lean into my own way of "consuming" art. For me, it was less about gaining knowledge, that is, the reading of descriptions or walking around a gallery in a logical order, but thinking about what feelings were evoked by looking at something or just being consumed sensorially by the thing you are looking at which means I often walk around these places nomadically. Most weekends, especially in winter, I spend Saturdays in galleries, museums or exhibition spaces. I think the cost of these places is still hugely inaccessible. My favourite exhibitions have been the Yoshitomo Nara (my most favourite artist in the whole world) and Ai WeiWei (an exhibition where I read every description, and it was the most emotional exhibition I have been to). All this is to say, I love looking at stuff and I always buy the exhibition books and my wellbeing is supported by looking at stuff.

Listening to music

You have probably experienced the impact music can have on your mood. I wrote above about singing; this is about listening to music. I have songs that I turn to that make me feel joyful, and others that make me cry. Harvard Health looked at a study in 2020 exploring the impact music can have on the brain. The survey suggested people who listened to music had higher scores for mental wellbeing and slightly reduced levels for anxiety and depression. The article explains how music activates a wide range of networks in the brain. In addition to activating the auditory cortex, it also stimulates the parts of the brain involved in emotion and memory, as well as the motor system, which enables us to pick up the beat and move our feet or bodies. They summarise that listening to music can support our wellbeing, stimulate our cognitive functions and enhance learning. Music can be a powerful reminder which can bring strong emotions. I know certain songs immediately transport me back to a certain time and place; some of these fill me with joy, others immediately bring me to tears.

Jamel talks about how listening to music supports him

Listening to reggae music, R&B, grime, rap and soca music from my culture brings me joy.

Listening to live music

Listening to music on our devices is excellent, but having the opportunity to hear music live is incredible. There is something about being among others, listening to the music being performed in front of you, that is incredibly special and a joyful experience. I have been fortunate to listen to bands in small and big venues, to hear choirs perform in beautiful churches and outdoors, and to be at festivals, hearing a band perform in front of an enthusiastic audience. Listening to music live gives an incredible boost to my wellbeing and a huge feeling of gratitude for the experience. There is something about the lingering memories that are important to me when listening to live music. I can still vividly recall watching Elbow at the Eden Project with our children; it was their first live gig, and this year, listening to Kate Rusby at a festival, being surrounded by friends, laughter, singing and dancing.

Moment for reflection

Do you have playlists you can turn to if you need an uplift or to relax? I have playlists for different moods and different situations.

Did you know?

There is a sea organ in Zadar, Croatia, where the waves flow over the marble steps, which have pipes inside them. As the waves wash over, they push air through the pipes, creating musical notes (this is on my wishlist to visit and swim there!). There is a link in the references which has a video of this.

Music and culture

When I was working on the book *Building Positive Relationships in the Early Years* with Jamel Carly Campbell (2022), we were discussing how music can be a great way to share cultures. Jamel describes how, when he worked in the Houses of Parliament nursery, he would play his favourite music, music that reminded him of his culture and family, which was often Bob Marley and Reggae. I loved this idea of sharing music from our homes and our cultures with the children we work with. It made me wonder how often we do that, but also how often we play music in the workplace to represent the cultures and homes that our children live in. Another idea Jamel shared was drawing to music, playing the children some music and getting them to respond to this through drawing or painting. I have used this a few times with children and in training sessions. It's a fun activity to do, and it's interesting to see the different responses to different types of music.

Kerry told me about how music supports her wellbeing

I turned 40 this year, and I decided to start going to gigs again, and that has been so much fun. Water soothes my nervous system; music fully activates it. I cry a lot to music, but that happy-sad feeling.

Books

I am also going to cover this in Chapter 6, but it feels wrong to have a section on engaging in culture and not include books. I love reading; I find it such a relaxing activity. Obviously, as a writer, I want people to engage in the written word. Thank you for doing just that! There is a term called Bibliotherapy, which recognises that books can support our mental health. The Pan Macmillan website has an article by Ali Roff Farar (2021) exploring how reading can support our mental health. Research has shown that reading can reduce our stress levels by lowering heart rate and decreasing blood pressure. They quote a study from the University of Sussex that found that reading for just six minutes has the power to reduce stress levels by 68%. It would appear that any reading can support your wellbeing; it doesn't have to be a novel, it could be non-fiction, poetry or essays. I have read a lot since childhood. I remember as a child loving how I could lose myself in a book; my family life was not always easy. My Mum has bipolar, and it was a turbulent experience, but reading a book meant I could block all that out. I'm aware this is still one of my big go-to's as a way of finding some peace, calmness and quietening my mind.

The year 2026 has been set as a national year of reading, supported by the National Literacy Trust and the Department for Education. The aim is to reconnect people of all ages with reading and to help people to see it as a relevant and rewarding activity.

This year (2026) has also seen the launch of a new research project with The University of East London, led by Dr Sam Wass, which will explore how shared reading can reduce stress, strengthen social connection and improve mental wellbeing.

A number of people I spoke to about their wellbeing tips mentioned books and reading as things that brought them joy and helped their wellbeing:

Tamsin on reading and singing

Reading and singing bring me joy! I used to be in a choir; sadly, I now work lots of evenings so can no longer attend, but I still love belting out the hymns at church every week and singing along to the radio as I cook or drive!

I love reading fiction and sharing recommendations with my children, as they're all teenagers and we like similar themes. My favourite author at the moment is Laura Wood, a romantic historical fiction writer, but I can't resist a good Lee Child page turner either!

Sarah on reading

Reading is my greatest pleasure. My degree was in English literature, and I love to be transported somewhere else. I don't just read critically renowned authors, and I'm happy to speed through a well-written thriller that leaves me breathless! I always, always have a book with me.

A variety of books

Reading doesn't have to be about reading a huge book or the latest Booker prize; many books are short stories or novellas. Novellas are longer than a short story but shorter than a novel. These can feel a lot less daunting, especially if it takes you a while to read or you don't have much time to read. Reading also doesn't have to be about reading fiction; there is a growing range of non-fiction books on a huge range of subjects. I have friends who find it hard to sit and read lots of words, but they have discovered that graphic novels work for them.

Moment for reflection

What was the last book you read or listened to for pleasure? This doesn't have to be fiction.

Films/ theatre

Research has shown that attending the theatre can benefit mental health. The UK Theatre and the Society of London Theatre released some statistics in 2021, suggesting that it supports people's mental and physical health. Through interviewing theatre attendees, people reported how they were able to lose themselves in the production and switch off their overactive brain, they were able to relax, and it lowered anxiety. In my experience, watching a film can do the same, particularly when I go to the cinema and watch it on a big screen. In the section on stress, I mentioned the Nagoski sisters and how they suggest that having a good cry or a good laugh can be great stress relief. Films can be brilliant for this. I know there are certain films that I can watch that will always make me laugh or cry. At the start of January 2026, two new films came out based on books I loved. It can always be a risk seeing the film of a book you enjoyed; these films were fantastic. They were Hamnet, and H is for Hawk. Both films made me cry, not just cry, but weep! And there was something incredibly cathartic about this.

Sarah spoke about how going to the theatre supports her wellbeing.

Sarah on the theatre and galleries

I go to the theatre at least once a month, whether this is to see live music, comedy or a theatre show. I love to visit art galleries and museums. That physical impact when something moves you is so good for your mental health.

Conclusion

You may be someone who loves engaging in creative practice, or maybe someone has never quite found their creative thing. I hope this chapter has encouraged you to try something creative; you never know, it might bring huge joy, or you may discover a skill you never knew you had.

Ideas on how to incorporate this into early years practice and at home

- Look at your creative area and check to see how enticing it is. Do the pens work? Do you have a range of paper with different colours, sizes and types of paper? Do you have glue, sellotape or string readily available? Do you have other resources they can use to create with, such as boxes, wool, buttons, corks or sticks? At home, you might not have space for a creating area, but could you make a creating tub that your children can use, where you can keep the creative materials in one place?
- If you have never used clay, consider buying some to use or making some air-dry clay.

- Try the activity of listening to music and responding with drawing or painting. You can do this at home or in a setting.
- Find out about everyone's favourite books and share these ideas with one another. Compile a bookshelf with the children's favourite books on, and you could also do one for staff. Maybe you could use this as a lending library, maybe with a bookmark in each book saying this is [staff member name] favourite book.
- Make a playlist of favourite songs in the setting; you could involve children, families, and staff in this. If you have Spotify, Apple or Amazon Music, you can make a list and then share it with the families.

If you have

If you have 2 minutes, put some music on and enjoy listening to the track, maybe find a track that matches your mood. Try to focus on the music and how it makes you feel.

If you had 10 minutes, you could try to draw something that is in the room you are in. Find some paper and something to draw with. This isn't about it looking perfect, just a quick sketch of what you can see. Try not to overthink it and instead just draw freely.

If you had 20 minutes, you could try to read something. Maybe pick up a book you have already started or one you have been intending to start, or it might be an article in a magazine you have in the house or a book of poetry. Maybe make a cup of tea to enjoy while you sit and read.

If you had 40 minutes, you could try to explore your home or garden with your phone camera, look with an open mind and take images of what captures your attention.

References

Art Fund: https://www.artfund.org/our-purpose/news/first-of-its-kind-study-proves-positive-impact-of-art-on-the-body

Art Fund: https://www.artfund.org/explore

BBC: https://www.bbc.co.uk/culture/article/20210105-why-being-creative-is-good-for-you

Burns, P. and Van Der Meer, R. (2020). Happy Hookers: Findings from an international study exploring the effect of crochet on wellbeing. https://www.researchgate.net/publication/340433493_Happy_Hookers_findings_from_an_international_study_exploring_the_effects_of_crochet_on_wellbeing

Carly Campbell, J. and Mainstone-Cotton, S. (2022). *Building positive relationships in the early years: conversations to empower children, professionals, families and communities,* Abingdon: Routledge

Courtauld Gallery: https://gallerycollections.courtauld.ac.uk/object-p-1948-sc-276

City Lit: https://www.citylit.ac.uk/blog/how-to-start-drawing-a-beginners-guide

Clare Day: http://www.claredayceramics.com/

Cross-stitch: https://www.thesprucecrafts.com/five-basic-stitches-in-cross-stitch-983962

Embroidery: https://www.thesprucecrafts.com/get-started-with-embroidery-1177438

Gregory, D. (2006). *The creative license.* London: Hachette

Goodbye June: www.youtube.com/watch?v=vlDoYSWCuzQ

Haidt, J. (2006). *The happiness hypothesis,* London: Cornerstone

Harvard: https://www.health.harvard.edu/blog/why-is-music-good-for-the-brain-2020100721062

Hand sew: https://www.thesprucecrafts.com/learn-stitches-and-hand-sewing-projects-2978472

Just One Thing: https://www.bbc.co.uk/programmes/articles/2VZPZmq2pRSMT2YHWbQdW7/why-singing-is-good-for-your-body-and-mind

Love craft: https://www.lovecrafts.com/en-gb/

Lost words: https://www.thelostwords.org/lostwordsbook/

London Theatre: https://officiallondontheatre.com/news/how-theatre-can-benefit-your-mental-health/

Luke Jerram: https://www.lukejerram.com/

Mental Health UK: https://mentalhealth-uk.org/blog/why-creativity-is-important-for-your-mental-health/

National Gallery: https://www.nationalgalleries.org/learn/you-art-world/health-and-wellbeing

National Literacy Trust: https://literacytrust.org.uk/about-us/national-year-of-reading-2026/

Natural Voice Network: https://www.naturalvoice.net/

Oxford University Research: https://www.ox.ac.uk/research/choir-singing-improves-health-happiness---and-perfect-icebreaker

Olafur Arnaulds: https://olafurarnalds.com/works/

Roff Farrar, A. (2021). Bibliotherapy and ways that reading can change our brains. https://www.panmacmillan.com/blogs/lifestyle-wellbeing/mental-health-benefits-reading-bibliotherapy

Sewing machine: https://www.prima.co.uk/craft/sewing/g60480188/how-to-use-a-sewing-machine/

Sing for Happiness: https://www.bbc.co.uk/news/articles/cdxy1ee5q9ro

Tate and slow looking: https://www.tate.org.uk/art/guide-slow-looking

Tate and families: https://www.tate.org.uk/visit/families-at-tate

The Indian Block Print Co.: https://www.theindianblockprintco.com/pages/home

UEL shared reading research: https://www.uel.ac.uk/about-uel/news/2026/january/uel-leads-queens-reading-room-shared-reading-research

Woman's Hour: https://www.bbc.co.uk/programmes/articles/3Zyf1xpVz2C4HkY2YZrDLJK/writing-as-therapy-five-reasons-why-you-should-pick-up-a-pen-and-paper-for-your-wellbeing

What Works Wellbeing: https://whatworkswellbeing.org/resources/creative-pathways-to-personal-wellbeing/

World Health Organization: https://ncch.org.uk/uploads/WHO-Scoping-Review-Arts-and-Health.pdf

Yuup: https://www.yuup.co/

Zadar sea organ: https://earthlymission.com/zadar-sea-organ-croatia-sound-music-listen/

6 Rest

In this chapter, I am going to explore what rest is, why we need it and the different types of rest that we can engage in. Rest is different from sleep, although I am going to look at sleep also. I think rest is often misunderstood, with many people assuming rest means having to totally stop, and often, people say to me they don't have time to stop and rest. I'm hoping this chapter will offer some ideas around the different ways we can rest.

Moment for reflection

Just for a moment, think about how you feel about rest. When you read the word rest, what comes to your mind?

Rest is something we all need to weave into our lives. Rest doesn't have to be doing nothing, although sometimes that is the rest that works for us in certain moments. Rest is about doing something restorative, something that relaxes you and that leaves you feeling refreshed afterwards. Doing something restful is an intentional act. We are all different, and we all find different things restful; it's about knowing ourselves and understanding what we find restful.

I wonder if the idea of resting can sometimes make us feel guilty. We live in such a driven society, where there is huge emphasis on doing and achieving, and to rest can sometimes be viewed as being lazy or may make us feel guilty that we are not doing all the things we should be doing. The

DOI: 10.4324/9781003717591-7

counterargument to that is we could view taking rest as topping up our energy banks, which then enables us to do all the things we need to do.

In 2016, there was a large piece of research based on studying rest, which was conducted in collaboration with the Wellcome Trust and Durham University; the BBC radio show All in the Mind was part of it, as their presenter, Claudia Hammond, was on the research team. They formed a multidisciplinary team which included historians, poets, artists, psychologists, neuroscientists and a geographer. They were based in Central London and called themselves the Hubbub team. In her book, Claudia describes how they chose their name: it acknowledged that for many of us, *"the hub and bub of life, the hurly burly, drowns out peace and quiet and the chance to rest"*.

For two years, they studied rest. As part of the research, they created an online survey called the Rest Test, which was launched from the *All in the Mind* radio program and *Health Check* on the World Service. Approximately 18,000 people from 134 countries participated in this survey, which was the largest conducted at the time on the subject of rest. You can find a write-up of this in a chapter titled *The Restless Compendium: Interdisciplinary investigations of Rest and Its Opposites* by Claudia Hammond and Gemma Lewis (2016). In the first part of the survey, the participants answered questions about how much rest they get, how much they would like and what activities they find most restful. In the second part of the survey, they answered questions measuring personality, wellbeing and the tendency for the mind to wander. For part of the survey, participants were given a list of words which best described what rest meant to them. The most commonly chosen words were:

Relaxing, peaceful, calming, comfortable, recuperative and sleep

Although a small number of people chose words such as:

Rare, stress-inducing, anxiety-inducing, guilt-inducing

Interestingly, more women picked the second set of words than men. The participants were also asked to pick from a list of 25 activities which they found most restful. The list of activities was:

Reading
Sleeping or napping
Looking at, or being in, a natural environment
Spending time on my own

Listening to music
Doing nothing in particular
Walking
Taking a bath or shower
Daydreaming
Watching TV
Meditating or practising mindfulness
Spending time with animals
Spending time with friends/family
Making/drinking tea or coffee
Creative arts
Gardening
Travelling on long journeys
Engaging in physical activity
Chatting
Drinking socially
Eating
Sexual activity
Running
Grooming
Thinking about the past

Moment for reflection

Take a moment to have a look at the list above. Are there things on this list that you find restful?

The results of the survey showed the top ten activities people found restful were:

1. Reading
2. Spending time in nature
3. Being alone
4. Listening to music

5. Doing nothing in particular
6. Going for a walk
7. A hot bath
8. Daydreaming
9. Watching TV
10. Mindfulness

As part of this two-year project, they produced an exhibition, poems, academic papers, a musical composition and Claudia Hammond wrote a book called *The Art of Rest* (2019). Her book explores each of the activities in the top ten. One of the things she noted from the survey was that the participants who said they felt fully rested had wellbeing scores twice as high as those who said they felt like they needed more rest.

I'm going to explore some of the top ten in a little more detail. You will notice some of them have already been covered in previous parts of this book, so I won't cover those again.

Reading

I'm not surprised that reading was number 1 on the list. I mentioned in Chapter 5 how much I find reading offers me the opportunity to switch off. This year, my friend and I set ourselves the challenge of reading around the world, basically trying to read a book that is set in every country. It will need to be continued in 2026, as I am writing this, we are almost at the end of 2025, and I have read books from 127 countries. I adapted it slightly as I have included England, Wales, Scotland and the Scottish islands as separate countries.

We have been using a free app called Mark O'Travel. It isn't a reading app, but it enables you to track your travels around the world and it colours in the map each time you add a country; I ticked to include other territories, which increases the places I can add. According to my map this morning, I have covered 73.6% of the world in reading this year!

My other adaptation in this is that I have included audiobooks on my list, which has enabled me to read/listen to many more books. The books I have been reading have mostly been from charity shops, borrowed from friends and from the library. I discovered this year that the library also has an app for borrowing audiobooks, it is called Borrow Box. Anyone in the UK can use it; you will need to sign up online with your local library, and then you can access free audiobooks, ebooks, and e-magazines. I have mainly been listening to audiobooks while driving between schools and nurseries. I have discovered this is an excellent way to help me switch off and find some moments of calm. Often, I leave school with my head full of what I have just been doing, seen or heard. By listening to an audiobook between visits, it helps me to find some calm, switch off from whatever is filling my head, and enables me to arrive at the next setting, feeling ready to switch to the next child or setting. I am sure that listening to audiobooks has helped my stress levels this year.

One of the joys of doing this challenge is that it has encouraged me to read books I would never normally read. I had my go to authors that I would often read, and favourite genres. This challenge has helped me to discover many different writers and places to read about. My big find this year, which many will have discovered before, is the author Elif Shafak. The first book I read of hers this year was *There Are Rivers in the Sky* (2025), which was my favourite book this year. I have bought it for several friends and family, and I have since read another two of her books.

Did you know?

New research by Sam Wass is showing us that when we are reading to a baby, our brains are synchronising, two brains beating to the same rhythm at the same time. They think these moments help early language development, help with emotional understanding and awareness and also help promote relaxation.

Being alone/solitude

I know that for some people, being alone is not restful or good for their wellbeing. We know that there is a rise in the number of people who feel lonely. However, increasingly, there is a recognition of how solitude can be beneficial for some of us. There has been a rise in books looking at solitude and the benefits of being alone; one of these is the book *The Science and Power of Being Alone* by Netta Weinstein, Heather Hansen and Thuy-Vy T. Nguen (2024), which acknowledges that the idea of solitude and being alone is not new (think back to hermits, monks and nuns). However, what is new is scientifically researching being alone or solitude. The three authors of the book mentioned above worked on a research project called the *study of solitude,* and their book explores their findings in this new scientific research. They recognise that finding solitude today is often different to how it was centuries ago, and not many of us want or can spend endless time on our own in the middle of nowhere! They recognise that there is what they describe as a middle ground from no solitude to total solitude; they describe this middle ground as *garden-variety solitude, happening every day to regular people.* They feel this is an important but oftenneglected space in research. For their research, they gathered information from thousands of research subjects across the world, across genders and socioeconomic backgrounds. From their interviews, they found people describing different types of solitude.

Complete solitude: The researchers describe this as the area that is more commonly looked at (think hermits), completely away from everything or everyone. However, they found that very few people they studied talked about this.

Private solitude: they describe this as a down-to-earth version of complete solitude. A space where you can do whatever you want, for example, read quietly, watch TV, play music loudly or sit quietly. A place we don't have to think much, or do anything in particular. In their research, they found people who described themselves as caregivers and empathetic particularly wanted this kind of space where they were free from other people's emotional baggage. When I read that, it made so much sense to me.

Companionate solitude: this is about solitude with another person we have a close connection with. This may be a partner/spouse of another person we have a close connection with. People talked about within that company having the freedom to turn inward and connect with themselves. Another description of this is partners-in-solitude, this would be spending peaceful activities in nature, at home or travelling with another person, being in the same space, engaging in the same thing, but in a peaceful way.

Public solitude: Some participants discussed public solitude, which is a psychological, not physical, separation, a way of being alone in public while with others. Some examples people gave of this were being on silent retreats, while others were around, but they weren't engaging with them. Or sitting/being among people and just being silent, watching what is happening around you (think of public transport or sitting in a park). One of the examples they shared was from a 65-year-old woman called Grace, who described her experience of swimming in the *silkiness of an open pond, where she enjoys the deliciousness of the activity and being alone among other swimmers.* That really resonated with me.

Did you know?

In medieval times, there were Anchoresses, who were religious women who chose to live by themselves in a small space called an anchorage, which was often attached to a church. The most famous one in England is Julian of Norwich

Moment for reflection

How does the idea of solitude make you feel? Some people have a longing. If it is something you think helps you, can you weave some times of solitude into your week?

A hot bath

I was amused to see that one of the top ten was having a hot bath. One of the people who offered me their wellbeing tips for this book was Kerry, who mentions having a hot bath as a way of helping her stress levels:

Baths. *I take baths as much as I can. I am not sure why, but just having a bath makes me feel safe.*

And I share this feeling, I love having a hot bath, I find it is such a good way to help me calm down, destress, and find some peace. While researching for this section, I discovered that bathing culture is a big part of Japan. It has been a centuries-old tradition of communal bathing, being both a spiritual and communal practice. As well as bathing in natural hot springs, which are located outside, these are called onsen. In the cities, they also have bath houses, which are called sentos. They have been set up for people to cleanse their bodies, relax and unwind. Apparently, it is common for people to go to these in the evening before going home to bed. If you are planning on visiting Japan and going to one of these (it is on my bucket list!) there is a useful guide on the Trip to Japan website on bathing culture and what to expect.

I often make a variety of bath salts and bath bags to go in my bath, and if I am suffering from a cold, I have a specific cold/flu bath salt recipe, which is so comforting. Below are three bath recipes:

If you don't have a bath or don't like taking baths, you could do a foot soak. Fill a bowl with warm water, and add some of the calming bath salts mentioned below.

Calming bath salts

Ingredients

1 tub or jam jar
Epsom salts or magnesium salts
Sweet almond oil/ coconut oil
Lavender essential oil

Instructions

Pour the salt into your tub/jar, almost filling it.
Add 3 tbsp of oil.
Add 12–15 drops of lavender oil.
Mix together.
Fill the bath and add 1–2 spoons of the salt into your bath.

Bath teabag

Ingredients

1 small muslin bag or disposable empty tea bag (you can buy these on Amazon)
1 tbsp dried petals, e.g. lavender/calendula/chamomile/rose
2 tbsp dried oats

Instructions

Add the oats and petals to the bag.
Tie the bag and place it into the hot water.
The oats in this recipe make the bath water feel very soft, and by using a bag, you don't have the problem of cleaning up the petals and oats at the end of the bath. You can empty the contents into the food recycling, clean and reuse the bag.

Bath salts for a cold

1 tub or jam jar
Epsom salts
3 tbsp sweet almond oil or coconut oil
Eucalyptus essential oil, tea tree essential oil, rosemary oil essential oil

Instructions

Pour the salt into your tub/jar.
Add tablespoons of oil.
Add around 5–7 drops of each oil into the salt.
Mix together.
Fill the bath and add 1–2 spoons of the salt into your bath. The oils will help with your breathing if you are full of a cold, and the Epsom salts are supposed to help an achy body.
If you're using an essential oil, make sure you get pure essential oil and not blended, also check if you have health problems or if you're pregnant before using.

Day dreaming

I love it that daydreaming was in the top ten. I was a child who spent a lot of time daydreaming and was continually picked up for it in class. Scientists have been looking at the idea of daydreaming and refer to it as mind wandering. This is the brain's natural state. The idea is that if you allow your brain to wander without chasing each idea, then this can be restful (this is one of the things you are encouraged to do while doing a mindful meditation). Some people find daydreaming helps with creativity or ideas. Over the years, I have been involved in several collaborative creative projects with my husband and friends, and all the ideas for these have come about from one of us daydreaming, often while in the bath! For some, sitting with thoughts can be a difficult area, especially if you're someone who ruminates over things, playing a scenario over in your head repeatedly. This can be a stressful experience and not restful. If ruminating is something that you struggle with, mindfulness can be incredibly useful for that.

Watching TV

I was really pleased to see this category in the top ten! I think this can often be a guilty pleasure for many. I absolutely agree that spending endless hours in front of the TV is not great, but sometimes there is a total joy and relaxation in watching TV. There is something about being able to lose yourself in a great drama or comedy, where you become so taken with it that you forget everything else. My top watches this year have been Slow Horses on Apple TV and Blue Lights and Rebel Women on iPlayer, and I am keenly awaiting season 4 of Bridgerton which is to be released on January 26, just as I am finishing this book, so a perfect way to celebrate. Living in Bath, I love spotting all the places they have filmed.

Mindfulness

There is a growing recognition of how beneficial mindfulness can be to our wellbeing. Mindfulness is about being present, noticing what is going on around us, inside us, helping us to stop and be aware. I mentioned mindfulness briefly in Chapter 1 as a stress release, and linked to the apps that are useful and an eight-week course. I think it is interesting to view mindfulness as part of a restful practice. I tend to dip in and out of mindfulness practice, but when I am having a stressful or difficult time, it is a practice I always pick back up, and it is restful, even if it is just a ten-minute meditation or a small noticing exercise. In those moments, it brings me a sense of rest. Many schools and nurseries now use some mindfulness practice with their children. I think if we are using mindfulness with children, it's important that we do it alongside them to model how to do it and the show importance of mindfulness.

On the NHS website, there is a useful introduction to mindfulness page, which includes a video featuring psychologist Dr Becky Spelman explaining mindfulness and its benefits, particularly for individuals experiencing low mood, anxiety, stress or poor sleep. Mindfulness can help us be aware of the moment we are in, allowing us to focus on our surroundings, the environment we are in and how our body is responding. Mindfulness is often described as the three C's: Curious, Compassion and Calm Centre.

Curiosity

Having curiosity can help us when we are experiencing difficult times; we can be curious about how we are feeling, how our body is reacting and how we are responding.

Compassion

It is about learning to be compassionate to ourselves (this is written about in Chapter 1), making sure that we are speaking kindly to ourselves and being gentle to ourselves.

Calm centre

Having a calm centre is about being able to stand back from the situation to try and view things afresh. Mindfulness teachers talk about imagining you are viewing the difficult situation through a telescope, being a step removed. This can help you to feel calmer.

Below are two micro mindfulness exercises you might like to try.

Noticing mindfulness exercise

You can do this inside or outside, just for a few minutes.

Find something natural to focus on, maybe a leaf/flower/shell or look out of the window at the sky.

Really look at the object.

Notice what you see, the colour, shape and any markings, the texture.

Just observe and ask yourself what I can see.

Mindful eating

This is an exercise often used in mindfulness courses, traditionally with a raisin, but to be honest, I find raisins so disappointing! When I use this in my courses, I offer berries and chocolate buttons, but any small item of food is fine (I am sure there are very good reasons for using a raisin, and this might be your preference).

Take a piece of food and hold it in your hand.

Look at it, really look at it, noticing the texture, the size, any variation in it.

Smell it.

Notice how that makes you feel, what is the reaction in your mouth and mind.

Now put it in your mouth and hold it there for a few moments.

Notice how that makes you feel, what is the reaction in your mouth and mind.

Now eat it slowly.

How did it taste? Better than you expected?

I really like both of the above micro mindfulness exercises, and they are both ones you can use with children. They can bring you a tiny moment of slowing down and calm.

Mindfulness is not a new idea; there has been an ancient practice seen through meditation, which has long been part of Hinduism, Christianity, Islam, Judaism and Buddhism. The mindful practices we see today have been created drawing on these ancient practices and formed in a way that you don't have to engage in the religious part of it.

The 7 types of rest

I am now going to explore an idea from Miranda Hart on rest. She may not be the first person you would think of for turning to in a wellbeing book, but her book, *I haven't been entirely honest with you* (2024), is full of useful wellbeing thoughts and tips. In the ten years before she wrote the book, she found out she had Lyme disease in childhood, which had led to many health difficulties over the years and then culminated in ME, or Postviral Fatigue, as it is also known. From this, she became bed-bound and needed to completely rethink how she lived and how she did wellbeing. One area she looks at is the 7 types of rest. She suggests that there are seven types of rest:

Physical
Mental
Emotional
Creative
Spiritual
Sensory
Social

Physical rest: this could be sleeping, napping, physically stopping, maybe through sitting down and people watching, or looking out the window. It's the time when you are not pushing your body or mind.

Mental rest: These are those moments when you don't have a task, you don't have to think about something specific. You can let your mind wander, daydream.

Emotional rest: this is about being in touch with your emotions, being aware of what you are feeling and allowing yourself to cry if you need that or laugh lots.

Creative rest: this is about engaging in something that is creative and playful, allowing yourself to be completely in the moment of the creative activity, where you're not thinking about anything else.

Spiritual rest: this will be different for everyone. For some, this is the active engagement in a spiritual practice or mindfulness/yoga, or it may be the experience you get from being in nature. Miranda describes it as "finding the awe and believing there's something that is loving and for me" (2024, p. 307).

Sensory rest: for this, she means having time away from stimulation, such as sensory stimulation that we might get from being on devices, and so on. However, I would include in that choosing to engage in something that is sensory can be restful, for example, having a hot bath, planting seeds/plants in soil. I often find that if I engage in a sensory activity, I find it very restful.

Social: for some, this will be having time away from people, particularly introverts who find they need time away from others to recharge, but for others, it will be time with people they find restful.

When I first read that list, I found it really helpful, not just for myself but also in helping me to understand a little more about our youngest daughter's experience, who has ME. I found it helpful to know there are a variety of types of rest, and at different times we need different types of rest. You can also see how they largely fit with the top ten list that came from the Rest Test survey.

Moment for reflection

Looking at the 7 types of rest, are there things you can think of that fit these areas for you? Sometimes it can be helpful to come up with a list of things you find restful, as a reminder when you need rest but you're too tired to think what to do.

Sleep

I am going to end this chapter by looking at sleep. Although sleep is different from rest, it is an important part of our wellbeing and this seems to be a good chapter to look at in more detail. Sleep is one of those areas that people can get particularly concerned about. It's not unusual for people to have difficulties with their sleep. There have been figures about how much sleep we should get, although doctors and scientists do say we should hold those lightly. The NHS guidance is around 7–9 hours for an adult a night. Different situations will impact our sleep; our age, health and personal situations can all impact the sleep we get.

We know there are some situations where our sleep will be impacted. If you have young children, you may be a carer, you maybe peri-menopausal/menopausal or you may have an illness that is impacting your sleep. But there are other times when our sleep can be disrupted, and it's not clear why.

We need sleep to repair or restore our bodies and minds. We can manage for short periods with sleep being disrupted, but if it goes on for an extended period, it can leave us feeling physically and mentally unwell.

Did you know?

In the 17th century, getting up in the middle of the night was normal; people slept in two segments, with an hour or two between them. The gap in the middle was used for reading, praying, having sex or socialising.

Sleep tips

There are some suggestions around sleep tips to support our sleep. Some of these are:

- Maintain a pattern – try to go to bed and get up at the same time each day.
- Have the room you are sleeping in dark – some people find wearing a blackout mask helpful.
- Turn off devices an hour before you go to bed, this is to do with the blue light we get from phones/tablets.
- Limit noise – some people find earplugs helpful.
- Recognise that alcohol/caffeine/tobacco are all stimulants, and if we take these before bed, that can impact our sleep.

- Have the room at a cooler temperature: too warm, and it is hard to go to sleep (although I am currently writing this in the winter in Norway, while visiting my daughter and too cold isn't good either!).
- Have comfortable bedding; the feel of your bedding, how your mattress and pillow feel, can make a difference.
- Have a bedtime routine when you begin to wind down. This might include having a hot non-caffeinated drink, you may have a hot bath or warm shower, you may sit and read for a bit or listen to some calming music. This is all giving your body the message I am preparing for sleep.

If we think about how we prepare children for bed, how they need a bedtime routine that is calm and peaceful, ideally, it is exactly the same for us.

There are a few things I use regularly to support my sleep:

Bath salts (see recipe above under baths)
Reading a book before bed
Having a herbal sleepy tea
Using a sleep herbal bag under my pillow

Sleep herbal bag

Ingredients
Small muslin bag
1 tbsp of dried lavender flowers
1 tbsp of dried chamomile flowers
1 tbsp of dried hops
Tie the bag and place it under your pillow. You can buy all of these online.

Did you know?

When people used to pick hops (they are used in beer), they used to feel very sleepy from the essential oils released from the hops. They have been used in sleep remedies for years.

Reading our bodies

I think with all of this, it's about reading our bodies, knowing when we need to take rest and what might be the kind of rest we need in that moment or on that day/weekend.

Conclusion

I think rest can be underrated. I think knowing what we find restful and finding ways to incorporate this into our lives is so beneficial. I used to feel guilty for resting, but I don't anymore. Being able to sit in front of the TV or having a hot bath and know this is resting and doing my body and mind some good is fantastic!

Ideas on how to incorporate this into early years practice and at home

- If you don't have a space already, make a cosy reading corner.
- Do some cloud watching with the children. If it is dry, get a rug and lie outside on the floor, looking up at the clouds.
- Try mindful eating with the children.
- Make a calming water tray, put some warm water in it, and some lavender bubble bath, or if you are able to make this as something they can stand in and get them to notice how the warm water makes them feel.
- Use cosmic kids to do some mindfulness.
- Play some calming music and encourage 5 minutes of resting and listening.

If you have

If you have 2 minutes, you could try some mindful eating, find some berries or chocolate. Notice how you feel once you have eaten it.

If you had 10 minutes, you could sit looking out of the window, cloud watching, or noticing what is going on outside. Notice the colours you see, the textures and how it makes you feel.

If you had 20 minutes, you could try having a hot bath maybe some bath salts to add to the bath. You might want to listen to some relaxing music

If you had 40 minutes, you could try having some time in solitude, maybe go for a walk on your own without music on, or have some time in the house or garden without people around or devices on. For some, this may not be possible to do.

References

Bathing culture in Japan: https://www.triptojapan.com/blog/ultimate-guide-to-japan-s-bathing-culture-sentos-public-baths

Borrow Box: https://www.borrowbox.com/

Cosmic Kids Mindfulness: https://www.youtube.com/results?search_query=cosmic+kids+mindfulness

Hammond, C. (2020). *The art of rest*. Edinburgh: Cannongate.

Hart, M. (2024). *I haven't been entirely honest with you*. London: Penguin

Lewis, G. and Hammond, C. (2016). *The restless compendium: Interdisciplinary investigations of rest and its opposites*. https://www.ncbi.nlm.nih.gov/books/NBK453237/

NHS: https://www.nhs.uk/every-mind-matters/mental-wellbeing-tips/what-is-mindfulness/

Sam Wass brain synchronising: https://www.facebook.com/watch/?v=612550691869905

Weinstein, N., Hansen, H. and Thuy-Vy, T. (2024). *The science and power of being alone*. Cambridge: Cambridge University Press

Conclusion

I hope this book has offered some ideas, but maybe also some hope. As I finish this book, it is the end of January 2026; January always feels like a long, hard month. It's been grey and wet and gloomy. Work has felt hard, and I have been trying to find tiny glimmers of hope where I can, but that has felt tough sometimes. My windowsills have daffodils and hyacinth flowers and tomato and chilli seedlings on them, to remind me spring will be here soon. And this morning on my drive home from the pool, I was aware of the morning light appearing earlier, and that brought me some hope.

We know that working in early years and education can be one of the best jobs, with fantastic moments of fulfilment, fun and laughter, but it can also be exhausting, at times sad and sometimes we wonder what we are doing. Throughout the book, I have talked about the need to take care of ourselves, find things that support us and nurture us. As I said at the beginning, looking after our wellbeing and loving ourselves is not a luxury, it is essential.

I am going to finish this book with some examples of how people find joy. Experiencing joy is such an important part of wellbeing. When I asked people about how they support their wellbeing, a number of them wrote about experiencing joy, and I thought it would be a lovely way to end the book.

Alistair: *There are lots of things that bring me joy. The right people, good food, laughing (sometimes just searching online for something I know will make me laugh does the trick), the list goes on. I think the secret is to seek it out as well as waiting for it to happen.*

Emily: *My own children bring me great joy. Trying to slow down together at the weekend, going to the RUH pool or watching them enjoy their sports clubs. Also, lots of hugs and play with our rabbits together.*

DOI: 10.4324/9781003717591-8

Aaron: *Joy comes from little everyday things, sharing a meal with loved ones, laughter with friends and moments of creativity. I try to weave joy into my life by making space for these simple connections.*

Kathy: *I like reading a well-written cosy mystery book, getting to know characters and feeling like I've visited the place. Meeting with friends and just talking – even if I'm really busy! Or especially when I'm really busy!!*

Sitting watching the sea or the ocean, with sunlight sparkling. When the light comes through our window decal in the kitchen and throws all sorts of rainbows on the walls (Rainbow Hour – there's even a song I sing to it!). Christmas with family and friends, and downtime to be together with my boys.

Tamsin: *Reading and singing bring me joy! I used to be in a choir; sadly, I now work lots of evenings so can no longer attend, but I still love belting out the hymns at church every week and singing along to the radio as I cook or drive!*

Sonia: *I have mentioned it throughout, but what brings me joy is being in nature, if possible, swimming, and experiencing something that is a glimmer of awe.*

Thank you for taking your precious time to read this book. My hope with this book is that everyone would find something in it they wanted to try. I love sharing recipes and things I have made with people; maybe you'll try some of these and love them too.

Index

For Product Safety Concerns and Information please contact our EU
representative GPSR@taylorandfrancis.com
Taylor & Francis Verlag GmbH, Kaufingerstraße 24, 80331 München, Germany

www.ingramcontent.com/pod-product-compliance
Lightning Source LLC
LaVergne TN
LVHW050058140826
845500LV00029B/281

* 9 7 8 1 0 4 1 2 0 7 0 7 8 *